SEEKERS OF HIGHER TRUTH

SANDY STEVENSON

Seekers of Higher Truth

Sandy Stevenson

Copyright © 2024 Sandy Stevenson

Book cover art by Sandy Stevenson

Imprint: Independently published

Table of Contents

INSTRUCTION

This book uses words to describe concepts of universal truth. Words are a substitute until we can draw on the pure essence of truth found in spiritual knowing. Truth comes when we reside in the stillness of a loving space of Spirit that enriches our lives beyond measure. We have all had times when that sort of understanding defies logic and we are at a loss to explain how we know what we know. But how amazing life is once we are consciously aware of a higher picture to life when words become almost unnecessary.

Let us accept words for the value they offer. Our educational system is geared to rushing us through subjects without expecting us to understand the words or thoughts we are presented with. Yet the way to fully learn any subject is to understand the meaning of every word as we go. Sometimes we can think we understand a word that we are actually not really sure about. If we go past words we don't really understand, we can lose interest in what we are learning and even experience physical, mental or emotional reactions, such as tiredness (start to yawn), headaches, boredom, feeling stupid or being overwhelmed. If we experience any of these, we have probably gone past a word or words we didn't understand. We can usually correct this by going back to the last point we understood well. Then start reading again from that point and take care to understand every word we read.

Anyone can learn anything, as long as they understand every concept as they proceed. Applying this we are able to excel at anything. With this technique, we can rehabilitate a subject we abandoned long ago. We can also begin something new we may have once felt was too difficult. We all love moving quickly on to the next thing, but keep in mind it can benefit us greatly in the long term when we understand each point as we go. Or at least be aware when we only half understand something. The path to wisdom is to know as we go. With this book, perhaps you could make a note at the end of each section about any points you are unsure of. Even if there is only a slight doubt, it is valuable to go back and review points. When we go past things that are not crystal clear, it is difficult to achieve increased understanding. We could also note special points we wish to ponder or refer to later.

We each have a gift to be able to discern different energies and truth. We feel a resonance of harmony deep within when we are comfortable with concepts that feel true. Equally, we may feel ourselves rejecting things that do not resonate with us. To establish either, we only need to listen to our inner voice. We are all at different points of discernment in what we encounter and can accept, dismiss or put some things on hold for further clarity.

It is requested you use your inherent gift of discernment to all you read in this book.

PREFACE

We've each had a role to play in our own unique way in this amazing divine plan to raise Earth to a 5D frequency. Together we have created a new blueprint that consists of billions of pieces of Source coded mathematics and sacred geometry that has created a pathway of light for humanity as they release 3D and make way for 5D. As part of the blueprint, we adopted and worked through all human conditions (physical, mental and emotional), illnesses, events, traumas and held many roles in all social establishments and structures. We might not be able to say we are always exactly sure what we are doing or why, but we follow our intuition and our knowing and we get things done in our unique way. Our persistence and insistence to take steps that feel right for us has culminated in a mathematical blueprint that will ultimately take the population of Earth to a new existence. The consciousness of humanity is now shifting and the increased light helps them see what is possible for a future. New realizations will penetrate solid walls of long held fixed beliefs and much of what has previously been held as truth will be replaced by a higher perspective of reality.

We have done our light work in ways that felt right to each of us. This is important. For myself, and perhaps for many others, I needed to personally experience things to discover my truth. I feel that was my agreement; perhaps my part in the blueprint creation. To discover truth, I chose an experiential method over channelling, reading books or attending workshops. This route has assisted me to be able to discuss things in depth and helped a lot with workshops, articles and books.

I believe anything is possible and feel we are able to combine logic and research with intuition. Exchanging ideas with others is a great way to examine views we have not considered. I remain open to unproven possibilities and find that rather than automatically dismiss things outside my current reality, I can store ideas of merit to await confirmation.

This book offers a possible higher perspective of the physical universe and the soul's journey from source as it wends its way through many dimensions and realities in a magnificent creation of wonder and awe.

What is written in this book is a view, a perception based on my experience in the universe and the knowing I gained from those experiences. It arises from our own ability to know and what the universe gives us for which I am deeply grateful. I have sought to keep concepts in the simplicity of truth. Hopefully, some points can offer additional understanding of this great adventure we willingly undertook, which certainly at times seems confusing and makes little sense. But magic happens as we begin to understand the overall concept of what exactly we are involved in and our collective roles as creators. We start to make sense of the apparent chaos and disorder and awaken to the perception of the incredible perfection that involves every molecule of existence.

I've tried to write only what I am able to stand by based on experience of sensing, perceiving, seeing, feeling and knowing what I found to be true. Nothing is written from a place of ego. We are all creators with spiritual abilities and can do anything if we consider we can. The problem is many people don't acknowledge themselves as spiritual beings or trust their inherent amazing abilities. Some points made are simply a statement without a solution, intended to encourage you to discover your own abilities. The term past lives is used because it is an easier way to grasp the idea of parallel lives, which is more accurate but harder to comprehend. All lifetimes occur in the same moment of existence.

I mention a few experiences I've had just to show how I arrive at points I write about. This can remind us we are all capable of amazing things.

In the points, I refer to golden balls that stabilize us in the universe, because I actually experienced it. Forty years ago, after an encounter, my body was feeling very out of balance. Looking for the reason, I found dislodged etheric golden balls and sensed the purpose for them and what had occurred. I rebalanced them into a perfect triangle and my body imbalance was immediately corrected. We often think we need special abilities to do something like that, but every soul can easily do such things.

I give a possible handling if the universe disappears because it happened to me and took me a couple of years to work out as I didn't have a blueprint. I mention the love of twin flames because I was lucky enough to experience it very briefly in the physical realm in this incarnation. I make points about ascension because I went through the process of replacing a carbon body with crystalline light and returning to source and finding the strength needed to be willing to leave and recommit to my task and agreements on Earth. That situation involved a lot of learning to function from viewing an almost transparent light frequency of 5D while re-establishing myself back in 3D. Living on light is mentioned because I did it for a long time.

I speak of Atlantean bodies because in the early 90's I needed to etherically recreate my original very tall Atlantean body to be able to enter codes to access the main Atlantean crystal now at the bottom of the Atlantic ocean, in order to filter out misinformation placed there long ago. We all carry codes. Some carry billions of mathematical codes in their field. It is something we generally don't need to be consciously aware of. I do, as it is an integral part of my work.

When working in the higher realms for a long time I experienced something quite incredible. I saw that every word and sound in existence has its own specific position within a mathematical grid. In fact, everything has its own place in that grid. I had previously glimpsed that many years earlier when I spotted I was storing other people's pain in a second etheric heart I had. I realized I had been doing this unconsciously for many years, when it felt right. From the time I became aware I was doing this, I observed that I would know exactly when to release a specific amount into a precise location in the universe. I understood the precise positioning meant the energy of it would have dissipated by the time it reached any nearby planet or species.

We all have an incredible ability to know and have used this on numerous occasions. Maybe we just don't acknowledge it enough. It's also interesting how easily we understand higher math out there, even if like me, we were not good at math in school. I've been closely following the time loss on Earth for 30 years and kept a record of it on my website, noting a regular slight loss with an occasional leap during mass world mediation activities.

There is much more I could share but am hoping it will be enough to remind us who we really are and that we only need to 'know' it, to be it.

Many of us have spent quite some time involved with Earth's ascension. It has brought us love, friendships, compassion, strength, growth and determination, alongside some difficulty, pain and loss that often accompanies 3D life. But we are almost finished. The pendulum has moved into the 100th monkey effect as information is being swiftly passed throughout the human collective consciousness. We are about to see a shift in awareness like never before. The manner in which this is unfolding is different than I think any of us had foreseen, but once we grasp the overall brilliance of what is occurring and see that it encompasses absolutely everything, including a fast forward in learning, growth and wisdom for humanity, we know we had a foolproof plan.

On Earth there is always a debrief undertaken after a mission. As above so below! We also have a gathering after a mission but ours is more of a major celebration at a banquet where we shall meet again the wonderful soul family we have shared this journey with and all the people we have loved deeply along the way. It may not exactly be a debrief. Perhaps more like a 'Wow, that was full on!'

I will see you at the banquet.

All points in this book are only my perception and may not be true for anyone else. I recommend everyone use their gift of discernment, intuition and knowing, to accept, dismiss or put aside for re-examination later.

With unconditional love,

Sandy Stevenson (Shantarn)

AND SO IT IS

We are taking a world into golden light to shine in brilliance and magnificence forever - a reflection of what can be achieved when a dedicated, diverse mix of beings from across the galaxies, come together in one voice, one strength, one united power, with immense compassion and an invincible determination in the pursuit of one united goal – to Create a New World of Love, Light and Harmony for all humanity.

The Earth is experiencing a unique universal change as this sector of the galaxy undergoes a major cosmic transition to higher frequencies of light. A higher divine picture overlays everything occurring on Earth. A world pushes itself past limited thinking and opens up in a magnificent realization of incredible interactions of differing realities and timelines and synchronicities. The veils of unseen worlds, wave lengths and dimensions begin to appear, as everything that is light becomes one.

We see perfection beyond physical senses, revealing billions of petals in a universal flower of sacred geometry, stretching across infinity of what is and is not. As each new section of the jigsaw falls into place, we are taken on the wings of eagles, soaring across vast oceans and over the highest mountains, with nights embedded in a zillion stars of other worlds and galaxies.

We know deep in our hearts we are on the most exciting and wondrous adventure possible. Worlds we never dreamed existed unravel before our eyes and we know we will never be the same. We find serenity in the infinite brilliance of a universal masterpiece. There is no doubt of the outcome for Earth. It is blazoned in gold across the universe, embedded in mathematics and written in the stars by the hand of Infinite Creation, recorded for all Eternity.

AND SO IT IS. IT IS DONE

Do not believe anything

because it is said by an authority,

or if it is said to come from angels,

or from Gods,

or from an inspired source.

Believe it only if you have explored it

in your own heart

and mind and body

and found it to be true.

Work out your own path,

through diligence.

Guatama Buddha

A student once asked of Buddha

Who are you?

Are you a God or an angel?

Neither, he replied

So, what are you?

I am awake, he replied.

WHAT IF

Everything in the universe

Is different

Than we believe it to be.

What if

We all have an inherent ability

To sense energy

And truth.

What if

It is important

To find our inner resonance

And dismiss anything

That does not resonate

As truth for us.

DEDICATION

A walker of universal skies

I sense a world of love I recognize

Indelible and flowing for eternity

I embrace it from the depths of my soul

Draw it close to hug it forever.

Shantarn

I reach beyond visible realms

to find the invisible

transporting me beyond space and time

into our special universe

recognizing who we are

as we touch and know again

the exquisite depths of infinite love.

Shantarn

TWIN FLAME

Come, toucher of deep in my soul

Let us leap together, beloved.

Freewheeling through time and space

In joy and laughter hugging the moon,

Shaping falling stars into new patterns

Sliding on the glimmer of galaxies rays

Dancing and leaping over planets

Looking for doorways of universes

Creating golden rainbows in our wake

My Love, my life, my world

All ways Always

For eternity

And beyond and beyond

Lighter and finer.

We have dreamed long

But we have dreamed well

You and I.

Sandy Stevenson - Shantarn

UNCONDITIONAL LOVE

Love without condition

I love you as you are, as you seek to find your own special way to relate to the world. I honour your choices to learn in the way you feel is right for you.

I know it is important that you are the person you want to be and not someone that I or others think you 'should' be. I realize that I cannot know what is best for you, although perhaps sometimes I think I do. I have not been where you have been, viewing life from the angle you have. I do not know what you have chosen to learn, how you have chosen to learn it, with whom or in what time period. I have not walked life looking through your eyes, so how can I know what you need.

I allow you to be in the world without a thought or word of judgement from me about the deeds you undertake. I see no error in the things you say and do. In this place where I am, I see that there are many ways to perceive and experience the different facets of our world. I allow without reservation the choices you make in each moment. I make no judgement of this, for if I would deny your right to your evolution, then I would deny that right for myself and all others.

To those who would choose a way I cannot walk, whilst I may not choose to add my power and my energy to this way, I will never deny you the gift of love that God has bestowed within me, for all creation. As I love you, so I shall be loved. As I sow, so shall I reap.

I allow you the universal right of free will to walk your own path, creating steps or to sit awhile if that is what is right for you. I will make no judgement that these steps are large or small, nor light or heavy or that they lead up or down, for this is just my viewpoint. I may see you do nothing and judge it to be unworthy and yet it may be that you bring great healing as you stand blessed by the Light of God. I cannot always see the higher picture of Divine order.

For it is the inalienable right of all life to choose their own evolution and with great love I acknowledge your right to determine your future. In humility I bow to the realization that the way I see as best for me does not have to mean it is also right for you. I know that you are led as I am, following the inner excitement to know your own path.

I know that the many races, religions, customs, nationalities and beliefs within our world, bring us great richness and allow us the benefit and teachings of such diverseness. I know we each learn in our own unique way in order to bring that love and wisdom back to the whole. I know that if there were only one way to do something, there would need only be one person.

I will not only love you if you behave in a way I think you should or believe in those things I believe in. I understand you are truly my brother and my sister, though you may have been born in a different place and believe in another God than I.

The love I feel is for all of God's world. I know that every living thing is a part of God and I feel a love deep within for every person, animal, tree and flower, every bird, insect, river and ocean and for all the creatures in all the world.

I live my life in loving service, being the best me I can, becoming wiser in the perfection of Divine truth, becoming happier in the joy of

Unconditional Love

Sandy Stevenson

OUR JOURNEY HOME

Now in Oneness - words and concepts stream from my heart to yours, filled with love and thanks to all who have shared this wonderful, strange, magnificent, challenging, magical journey, as together we travelled through parallel lives, nation to nation, gaining and imparting wisdom and anchoring the light of All That Is.

As I stand here, aware of my intimate world weaving its way beyond the senses, I reach into the past and pull forth from the fathomable depths that was Atlantis. A wisp of a recollection of our dream and undeniable truth of a continent of light, gracefully majestic in its perfection of beauty, sound and mathematics, forged from our ancient understanding and mastery of technology from eons past. Now a dream come true as Atlantis rises again to Ascension.

I thank everyone who has walked this journey with me. I thank all those who extended their hands in times we needed each other when the strain of the moment threatened to engulf us and who we were. Born from our strong desire to move forward to achieve our goal, we grasped each other, holding fast until danger passed. We assisted each other to take one more step until we could stride forth once again with heart strong and purpose renewed, strength of spirit prevailing, ready to accomplish all we set out to do so very long ago.

The entire third dimension reality on Earth is being revealed and truth experienced by humanity. As individuals become aware and reject energies they do not prefer, they step into their power and unify globally in Oneness, creating a magical world of light in the 5th dimension.

Together, standing in the strength of pure Divine light, having lived each moment, each day, each lifetime, we achieved our goal. We have brought about a new dawn, the Ascension of Earth and the final stages now play out.

May your heart and soul be filled with love and a deep sense of peace. May you be the person you truly are and lead by example with truth, integrity, compassion, understanding, honesty, a gentle heart and love.

To the amazing Light team on Earth - and the beautiful Cosmic Clan of friends and family who have shared love and laughter over the years as we exchanged views on how to set the world to rights and then watched divine order handle it way better, creating the most incredible awakening and dissolving of 3D reality. Thank you all for allowing me to be a part of your world. I am so grateful and love you all.

May the Source of Creation touch your wings and wrap you in golden light as you step with excitement into a new world of light and magical creation where dreams come true.

Sandy Stevenson

(Shantarn)

THE SOUL

What if every soul has at least one spiritual ability that benefits the world.

What if souls can telepathically communicate with all life forms, including other souls and nature, e.g. water, trees, animals.

What if everyone on Earth has free will and choice.

What if being responsible and acting in integrity aligns the soul with divine order.

What if there are no accidents because everything that happens is created from the soul's thoughts.

What if even choosing a non optimum path still enables learning and growth.

What if it is impossible to separate a soul from its physical body without the soul's agreement.

What if every soul has a light body they use beyond the 3D dimension.

What if a soul's light body is at the frequency of the soul's highest point of evolution.

What if a soul has an aspect of itself existing on every dimension it has evolved to.

What if there is no limit to the abundance a soul has in their life provided there is no need or attachment to it.

What if one reason a soul does not attract money is because that will not help its spiritual goal or the soul has a belief that prevents it receiving money, e.g. I never win money

What if a soul can increase its vibration by being grateful for life, breath and being able to experience.

What if a soul works toward a goal to remain balanced regardless of external circumstances.

What if many are losing their memory because they are swapping from mind memory to the higher vibration of intuitive 'knowing'.

What if over the years, as we merge with our I Am Presence, our eye focus goes through periods of adjusting and we may need reading glasses.

What if a soul learns by overcoming all limitation, the separation from source and loss of personal power.

What if wisdom is gained by overcoming limitation ad barriers.

What if the concept of beauty and ugliness are 3D beliefs and have no basis in truth.

What if the soul creator is capable of instantly reversing concepts of what is beautiful or ugly.

What if communication is the universal solvent.

What if it is a goal of each soul to realize it is complete without the need for anything or anyone to help it feel complete.

What if detachment, integrity, discipline, responsibility and love are integral to soul advancement.

What if ego curiosity gives way to spirit and the soul works on a 'need to know' basis.

What if souls who were dark witches in the past, reflect classic witch aspects in their current body.

What if the etheric subtle energy bodies that surround the physical body contain marks or scars of old injuries or conditions from past situations which can help them see unresolved situations.

What if spiritual beings of the 7th dimension or above are not permitted to enter 3D physical incarnation because their high frequency can raise the frequency of incarnated souls nearby.

What if using the prefix I AM in our affirmations connects us to source energy. I AM well.

Aura

What if souls have an auric energy field (aura) containing many colours around their physical body.

What if viewing the etheric field shows the condition of the physical body.

What if the size of the auric energy field reflects the soul's current energy capacity, with a larger field being stronger.

What if colour and sound are a vibrational frequency and each colour matches a specific sound.

What if colour can be positive or negative if a person has too much or not enough.

What if a soul can be adversely affected by wearing colours denser than the soul's frequency.

What if a soul can use colour, sound, light essences, positive thoughts, affirmations and high frequency technology to repair, heal and strengthen the aura on all levels.

What if we can replace colours missing from our aura by intuitively selecting colours of clothing.

What if heavy drugs, alcohol, major trauma or constant negative thoughts creates tears and holes in our aura.

What if negative entities can enter a soul's auric field through holes and rips in it created by the soul, causing bipolar, psychic conditions, psychic attack and severe emotional reactions.

What if we keep our auric field strong and intact by maintaining higher vibrations.

What if auras can be cleared of negative energy by strengthening the auric field, using decrees or by removing entities. See website Articles page.

What if negative thoughts and emotions drain colour from our auric field and cause imbalance and illness.

What if when we visualise light coming into our aura we need an intent for it to be the right mathematical frequency for us at that moment.

What if the clothes we wear absorb 3D energy from the environment, so it is ideal to wash them before wearing again.

Birth

What if the roles of parents, siblings, children and key people are arranged in a pre-incarnation plan.

What if sometimes we need to wait for a soul to complete its current incarnation in order to be included in our incarnational life plan.

What if there are no mistakes when choosing parents.

What if for about 3 months prior to birth, the soul is located near the body and in control of it.

What if the soul does not enter the body until just prior to birth.

What if a soul chooses the moment of birth to coincide with the position of planets that offer specific energies to assist souls achieve their goals. A soul wishing to learn balance and love in relationships may choose to be a Libran, being born when Venus is near Earth.

What if a baby has 6 weeks to abort an incarnation if major changes are made that will affect the soul's ability to achieve its goals. This is one reason for cot death.

What if the same soul may have been with us in other lives as a parent, work associate, sibling, partner, adversary or child.

What if a soul arranges incarnations of varying circumstances for experience and learning. Perhaps a beggar, king, rich, poor, male, female, a cripple, abandoned at birth or cast aside by society.

What if the there is a sequence of soul entry into a body, beginning with the lightest body first – the higher spiritual body, then the mental body, emotional body and finally the densest, the physical body.

Channelling

What if major discernment needs to be applied to all information received from anyone or any place, including channelling.

What if all souls channel in some form, whether it is light, healing, information or one of five types of telepathy.

What if we need to discern the resonance and level of any discarnate soul we are in contact with and use our gut knowing before accepting any claims made.

What if souls have an aspect of themselves on every level they have evolved to.

What if some discarnate beings who claim a specific identity could be a lower aspect of that identity.

What if discarnate beings are allowed under universal law to claim to be any identity because it teaches others discernment and intuition.

What if there is always free will and choice to accept or refuse channelled or telepathic communication.

What if, under no circumstance, should you do something told in channelling that does not feel right

What if any telepathically received information needs to resonate as 100% true before accepting it.

What if it is best to ascertain the level of any discarnate being we are in communication with.

What if a soul feeling tired or drained of energy after any communication, action or channelling usually means the action was not in divine order.

What if the 4th dimension contains many discarnate souls who make connections with incarnated souls for fun and control, often claiming to have access to higher truth.

What if some channelled information is for you to know about and not for passing on.

What if souls are sometimes tested by higher evolved guides by being given incorrect information to help increase the soul's intuitive abilities, discernment and mastery.

What if there was also a fake tunnel of light set up for those passing on, that caused some of lower awareness to loop into further 3D incarnations. It was dismantled by the Light Force in 2023.

Death

What if only the physical body dies and the soul is eternal, immortal and infinite.

What if we pre-choose the moment of death.

What if we pre-plan up to 6 exit points where we can leave the incarnation if we wish.

What if a soul reaching its final exit point is able to use universal process and protocol to extend their incarnation.

What if when the body dies, the soul joins with higher guides and a spiritual team to review their incarnation.

What if an incarnation review is always done to assess spiritual goals attained and examines what alternatives were possible in situations and where karma could have been avoided.

What if following the post incarnation review, aspects are taken into account when planning the next incarnation.

What if a soul can be coerced; convinced it is in their best interest ; given promises; a storyline; etc. to be persuaded to vacate their body.

What if the only judgement that can arise from committing suicide is made by the soul itself who reviews its life after it passes on and sees the other choices it could have made.

What if some suicides are a right action in divine order and part of the soul plan.

What if most suicides usually include a failure to keep some agreements due to their sudden departure, which may need addressing in the next incarnation.

Discernment

What if the ability to discern energy is a perception of spirit all souls have.

What if perception is an awareness of the energy of a person, place, object, product, thing, etc. Which gives us a choice to align with it or not.

What if when we judge an energy as being right or wrong, good or bad, it changes a higher spiritual perception into a lower 3D duality.

What if discernment is perhaps the most vital area on Earth at this time.

What if the vastness of the far reaching effects of discernment, both in its application or lack of it, are beyond imagination and comprehension.

What if we all truly commited to the practise of discernment, the resulting outpouring of Light could change the Earth in a moment.

Healing

What if every soul has the capacity and ability to heal itself of any condition.

What if life is a mirror that reflects what we have created.

What if a soul needs to be intuitive when choosing a healer or a spiritual practice.

What if healing is more beneficial when the patient and healer are from the same soul family.

What if intuitively choosing a healer with a similar frequency to ourselves can avoid compression or collapse of our auric field.

What if a healing circle works best if all are from the same soul family.

What if metal has positive and negative effects, depending how much is absorbed into the body. Too much or too little may not be beneficial, e.g. wearing the same metal jewellery for a long time.

What if nature provides essences from trees and flowers, etc. such as Bach Flowers, that reinstate positive energy vibrations to help any mental and emotional condition that humanity can experience.

What if positive thought and actions play a major role in health.

What if a soul can use colour, sound, light essences, positive thoughts, affirmations and high frequency technology to repair, heal and strengthen its physical and subtle energy bodies.

What if using vibrations of sound, colour and plant essences can balance emotions.

38

What if music that resonates with the soul is because it is in the same frequency band as the soul and can heal.

Human And Other Bodies

What if souls can have different types of bodies on other planets, such as synthetic bodies with easily replaced parts.

What if some life forms in the universe operate with a hive mentality and have a controller, similar to a hive of bees or ants.

What if a soul adopts different bodies for learning purposes or a rest, perhaps as an animal.

What if there are two main learning paths in the universe. One experiences through the elemental and angelic kingdoms and the other through human type forms.

What if many souls complete their learning obtained in the Angelic realms and move to being human for further experience.

Illness

What if an illness is a sign reflecting a specific underlying thought pattern that needs releasing. See 'You can heal your life' by Louise Hay

What if a specific thought causes a specific illness or condition.

What if a real or imagined loss anytime from 10 days prior to signs is the cause of a common cold.

What if individuals vary in their ideas of a loss, one considering a house burning down and another it may be their favourite pencil. It is the soul's consideration that the loss will lessen their survival.

What if locating the general area of loss progresses the cold to a faster completion, therefore increasing symptoms that would have occurred more slowly. E.g. I miss Mary.

What if locating the exact thought that created the illness removes the illness instantly. E.g. I miss Mary bringing me breakfast in bed.

Incarnation

What if prior to incarnating, a soul joins with their spiritual team of guides and plans out the next incarnation with its key roles and main events.

What if prior to incarnating, important events are pre-arranged to give the best chance of success of goals.

What if a soul's incarnational plan includes achieving specific spiritual goals, abilities and qualities.

What if incarnations are planned within our soul family and our core group, with souls who often take key roles, such as family, partners and friends.

What if everyone in your life is meant to be there for a reason.

What if the soul's incarnational plan includes achieving its spiritual goals, balancing karma and releasing anything that does not reflect the soul's truth.

What if a soul incarnates into a third dimension (3D) to become wiser and more loving from the many experiences offered in a duality existence; good/bad, positive/negative, right/wrong, north/south, male/female, etc.

What if life on Earth, or in any third dimension (3D), is a game with opposing sides – each side playing a role in the exchange and interaction of circumstances, limitations and barriers, designed to help us learn compassion, tolerance, understanding and love for all life.

What if a soul leaving an incarnation is so attached to that life they do not wait to reach the still place needed to plan their next incarnation but instead jump straight into a new incarnation without a plan. The soul often retains some memory of the previous incarnation. Such a reincarnation often doesn't help soul advancement.

What if when a soul attains what it needs to learn, it can stop attracting lessons and start to attract whatever it prefers.

What if upon entering 3D incarnations the soul forgets its goals, purpose, that it is spirit and a creator, so it can experience 3D events and gain wisdom. This process of forgetting is called the veils of maya.

What if we don't remember our pre-incarnational plan in order to gain from 'unexpected' events we learn to overcome.

What if the soul creates experiences and deliberately forgets it created it so it can learn from it when it suddenly appears. The apparency of time between a thought and the manifesting of the event assists this.

What if learning on Earth includes realizing that the intentions, thoughts and actions we send out into the world act like a boomerang and are returned as experiences.

What if occasionally an arrangement (often pre-arranged) is made between a soul and another (discarnate, more evolved) soul to merge temporarily with them to assist an important job they need to do in their divine role that will assist with energy, stamina and expertise. The merging is effortless and is experienced as an easier flow of life.

INCIDENTALS
Atlantis

45

What if the 31st October as celebrated by the dark symbology of Halloween, was the day Atlantis sank.

What if the evolved continents of Lemuria and Atlantis sank and some of their cities remain under the Pacific and Atlantic oceans.

What if the Bermuda triangle, known for the disappearance of ships and planes, occurs when a vortex is created at a specific mathematical degree hitting the apex of the main crystal that operated Atlantis and now is upright at the bottom of the Atlantic Ocean.

What if that main Atlantean crystal at the bottom of the ocean holds complete record of the history of Earth and its future.

What if many souls who were incarnated when Atlantis sank, incorrectly believes their technical research of scientific experimentation caused Atlantis to sink.

What if the cause of the Atlantis sinking was a result of welcoming other planet's travellers and failing to see the stealth of manipulation introduced. We are reliving Atlantis with a different outcome planned.

What if Atlantean bodies were very tall, ranging from 7 to 10 feet.

What if a tunnel system existed under the ocean that allowed Atlanteans to travel to other continents.

Galactic Federation

What if the Galactic Federation of Light helps keep order in the universe, assisting planets without interferring with their own evolution.

What if the Galactic Federation of Light assists the galaxy that contains Earth.

What if the Inter-galactic Federation of Light space fleet assists the rest of the universe.

What if there are 59 fleets of 4,600 ships in the Galactic Federation of Light.

What if some souls currently incarnated are also space fleet personnel in a parallel existence.

Animals

What if all animals have a soul and the less evolved animals have a discarnate soul that controls a group of animals, which is learning and growth for that soul.

What if one discarnate soul operates large groups of smaller species such as insects, ants, bees, etc.

What if most large animals are souls in their own right, such as elephants, giraffes, lions, etc.

What if many old souls are in animal form , including many cats, dogs and horses and sharing this last physical incarnation with people they love.

What if bottlenose dolphins and many whale species such as humpbacks, are highly evolved species from Sirius.

What if humpback whales are the floating libraries on Earth, holding all the history of Earth.

What if the veil between humans and the elemental kingdom of more subtle energies is vanishing, assisting humans to sense subtle energies and move closer to ascension.

What if a soul's awareness of the elemental kingdom will dissolve a major 3D barrier.

What if every soul can telepathically communicate with nature's elemental creatures and is able to request ants or wasps to leave an area as well as give warning to elemental beings of pending tree lopping, clearing or intense gardening.

Karma

What if karma is caused by the intent and undertaking of mental, emotional or physical actions that are not in alignment with the essence of the soul.

What if karma is the cause and effect consequence of imbalanced energy.

What if we can delay addressing karma for many incarnations.

What if we reach our final 3D incarnation and still have to finalize all outstanding karma, which can result in a soul experiencing traumatic events incurred for extended periods, especially in childhood.

What if souls who do not plan to address outstanding karma in the final incarnation may need to incarnate for as many incarnations as necessary to address the imbalance of energy.

What if we can accrue positive karma and pass it to others, where in divine order.

What if we sometimes take on other people's karma to assist them.

What if always acting in integrity ensures an increase of vibration and lessens the possibility of creating karma.

Learning

What if souls have free will to choose to learn through the consequences of their actions and make decisions based on their experience.

What if soul growth is obtained by following what intuitively feels right in each moment in the natural flow of divine order.

What if every event we experience or hear of means we have already chosen that as part of our reality.

What if lessons increase in intensity and frequency until we handle or release what we are being shown.

What if all we are really doing is letting go of anything not in alignment with the soul.

What if souls have an unseen etheric antennae that attracts what they need to learn.

What if our etheric antennae attracts people and situations that show us specific reactions we need to address and stops sending signals when a reaction is gone and no longer needs handling.

What if our greatest teacher is through relationships, often those we can't easily leave, such as family.

What if we can learn from ignoring our intuition and allowing the ego, thoughts and emotions to dictate our path.

What if truth can come from any source in any moment, a child, the spoken or written word, an animal, nature, art, object, person, music, silence, and observation of life.

What if lightness, fun, play and laughter create a higher vibration that assists the success of our goals.

What if laughter is a high vibration and more beneficial than serious contemplation.

What if a lack of confidence in self can encourage us to give our power to people we feel can do a better job.

What if an instant feeling of distrust or dislike when meeting someone can be karmic or a warning sign to move on.

What if life is a reflective mirror that constantly shows us what we need to learn.

What if personal growth is gained by letting go of everything that does not reflect truth of the soul.

What if guidance from inner knowing is senior to guidance from the ego, mind or emotions.

What if we need to trust the universal process and ourselves.

What if we allow and trust divine order and don't attach expectations or outcome of how we think the result should be.

What if raising our vibration helps us be less influenced by the outer world.

What if giving freely without conditions is a true path of the soul.

What if gratitude for everything is a state of awareness that raises personal light vibration.

What if raising personal vibration helps raise the collective consciousness of humanity.

What if stopping judgements helps free us from the 3D matrix.

What if receiving incorrect information assists us with discernment and wisdom.

What if it does not serve soul growth to be consciously aware of the purpose of events we create to learn from them.

What if we need to find the balance between being grounded and being aware of higher energies.

What if a failure to be grounded means we are not present in the moment and miss universal signs, appointments and often lose things.

What if we can intuitively know how many times to repeat a positive affirmation, e.g. 'I am well,' to transmute and replace opposing negative thoughts.

What if when we have to keep reminding ourselves to apply a spiritual aspect to life, it is because we have yet to integrate that concept into our being and are still holding it as a mental thought.

What if everything you feel, think or say, whether 'good or bad', has a profound effect and causes a constant alteration of your vibrational frequency.

What if you have an ability to view an uncomfortable incident that occurred in the past and mentally imagine it had a different outcome, which releases its negative energy.

What if blame, complaints, criticism, judgements and condemnation contain negative energy and reduce personal vibration.

What if when choosing to express fear with our words and actions, the universe responds to our creation and sends us what we feared.

What if having loving thoughts and actions means we receive love from the universe in forms we consider possible.

What if the difference between an affirmation and a decree is that an affirmation is repeating a statement to cause a reprogramming of a belief pattern and a decree is a one off statement or request registered in universal law.

What if we need to be intuitive and not believe what we are told, even by experts.

What if many people's lives are controlled by thoughts, ego or emotions instead of intuition.

Mathematical Codes Held By The Soul

What if every soul on Earth carries mathematical codes in its energy field.

What if mathematical codes carried by souls are exchanged with other souls and passed into the leyline grid system of Earth and many locations including sacred sites.

What if the greater the capacity of the soul, the greater the amount of codes it is able to carry in its energy field.

What if most souls are not usually aware of carrying and exchanging codes as it occurs automatically so as to minimise distraction from their soul purpose.

What if the main reason for a fast turnover of products is to help Earth's vibration as new products are made in the mathematics of a higher energy vibration.

Parallel Lives

What if a soul can hold different points of view, in different bodies, in different timelines, in parallel lives, all at the same time, each offering a completely different experience for the soul.

What if we are capable of keeping our parallel lives completely separate and unknown to us, avoiding confusion.

What if this is how a soul gains more experience quickly.

What if a soul start with just one incarnation and grows in ability to handle more at once.

What if parallel lives, often called past lives do exist, but are not really in the past. Instead they are all happening simultaneously in the present moment.

What if many people in our parallel lives are also in our current life.

What if it is possible, consciously or unconsciously, to recognise someone we know in a parallel life.

What if we use the term past lives rather than parallel lives because it is easier to understand.

What if many lightworkers and Starseeds have identities in other 3D parallel lives, each assisting Earth's ascension.

What if parallel lives increase our experience and wisdom.

What if someone you have a difficult learning relationship with in this incarnation, may also be your loving partner in a harmonious parallel life.

Reactions

What if the universe deliberately offers situations to trigger our unhandled stored negative reactions to help us become aware of what energy needs releasing.

What if we need to release dense energy patterns and negative behaviour in order to return to our true self.

What if choosing to ignore or release reactions means they will need to re-occur.

What if the signs showing what we need to release begins with us receiving subtle signs at a distance, perhaps hearing of someone else experiencing it or seeing something on TV we have a reaction to.

What if when we ignore the subtle signs we see, the universe brings them closer, stronger and they occur more often.

What if flooding our subtle energy auric field with light can help dissolve reactive emotions and thoughts.

What if our reactions, emotions, rigid thoughts and belief patterns all contain dense energy and we are unable to progress to higher frequencies with dense energy in our field.

What if it helps us release our reactions if we can identify the precise thought, pattern or emotion which creates more truth and makes it easier to transmute the energy.

What if there are usually more than one reaction that is triggered in an incident and we need to handle each of them.

What if we can release reactions that are present on the surface.

What if we can bring to the surface a reaction we are not currently feeling by imagining the situation that triggered it. Then flooding our aura with light to dissipate that energy.

What if when we have released all our reactions, we can get what we prefer in life rather than continuing to receive the lessons we need.

What if inner excitement is a sign we are on our most optimum path.

What if a feeling of excitement that shows our right path is often suppressed by overriding emotions, such as fear or doubt.

What if we have a gut knowing when we are on the right path.

What if we handle a specific reaction but don't realize it is gone and continue to address it and recreate it again.

Reality

What if everything in our world exists because we agree it is real.

What if a soul agreeing, past or in the present, to an idea, object, situation, product, event or the existence of anything, makes it possible to experience it in any form.

What if the reality that receives the most agreement and therefore the most energy, becomes the predominant reality in the life of a soul, nation or planet.

What if every situation in your life is there because you agreed it was possible. The more agreement you give it, the more real and the higher the chance of it occurring.

What if anything we can conceive as possible, is possible.

What if even the thought that something is impossible, also becomes part of our reality.

What if belief, faith, trust, and positive thoughts help dreams come true.

What if protection from negative influences is only necessary if a soul believes itself to be vulnerable.

What if the 4D astral plane has many souls who have died in 3D incarnations who believe they are still alive because what they see around them looks similar, unaware where they are is a bit lighter frequency of energy.

What if when you release your reactions, the universe rearranges itself to accommodate your new picture of reality.

What if we attract people with the same reality and beliefs as ourselves, which appears to confirm what we believe is true and makes us more certain we are right.

What if every person in your life is there because you attracted them for some form of spiritual growth, yours or theirs.

What if everything that happens to you or is done to you, occurs because you agreed it exists.

What if you are never a victim and always a creator.

What if we live most of our life through beliefs we adopted from family, friends, media, experience, books, society, movies, education, religion, race, tribe and beliefs handed down through generations.

What if sharing time with people of similar reality can be highly supportive during the transition of Earth.

What if mixing with people of different realities can assist us release judgements and reactions and learn.

Sleep

What if the soul replenishes itself during sleep by connecting to a higher energy source.

What if deprivation of sleep prevents the soul replenishing its energy.

What if not remembering what occurred during sleep is a deliberate choice made by souls before incarnating to ensure the soul is grounded, present and willing to re-enter its 3D role upon waking up.

What if the soul remembering the higher purpose for situations in its life would prevent learning from it.

What if meetings are held in the etheric realms during the night as needed for light teams to update their plans concerning their particular roles in the ascension of Earth.

What if during sleep a soul often examines situations in their life to gain a clearer perspective.

What if the timing of meetings held in the etheric at night are arranged in 3D timing to allow souls to wake up and sufficiently ground themselves in time to attend to daily incarnated activities.

What if the night meetings end at 3am, often resulting in waking up but we are able to easily go back to sleep if we don't protest waking up and don't start thinking.

What if night meetings are less frequent once plans are fully in place and progress discussions are not required.

What if a soul returning from sleep with knowledge that can assist its life then needs to intuitively act on it.

What if sometimes we wake up very aware of a place or situation that seems real, it can be a real location we just left.

Soul Cords

What if an invisible energy cord exists between souls, places and things that are connected for that soul.

What if cords exist between souls with a close bond and can be used to exchange energy and codes.

What if etheric soul cords vary in thickness and colour, signifying the strength of energy between two souls. A thin cord showing a lesser connection than a thick cord. A gold cord is a high soul connection and a silver cord is a connection maintained for teaching and growth purposes.

What if it can help to end an unwanted relationship if we imagine an etheric pair of scissors and feel or know where our connecting cords are around our body and cut them. There are often several or more.

What if souls have three large golden balls in a triangle in their etheric energy field, linked to points in the universe to help stabilize and balance the soul and maintain its ownership over its body while in human incarnation.

What if a major psychic encounter can cause an imbalance of a soul's etheric golden balls and a rebalancing of them is needed.

Soul Fragments

What if a soul is capable of fragmenting itself and locating in many places.

What if a soul whose body dies or it needs to leave a situation but wants to know the outcome, is able to leave a fragment of itself behind to observe.

What if scattered fragments a soul leaves around the universe reduce a soul's capacity to have its full attention in its present life.

What if a soul has the ability to retrieve all its fragments and become complete.

What if a soul who is permanently leaving 3D existence gathers all its soul fragments so it can leave as a complete soul.

Thought

What if it is thought by souls that creates the entire physical universe.

What if our individual thoughts create every interaction, every encounter and every event we experience in all dimensions but the thought is consciously made in higher frequencies.

What if we are able to find all our thoughts, whether in conscious or subconscious.

What if it is a thought precedes all illness, perhaps created long ago, and finding that thought can heal the illness.

What if everything we think, do or say impacts our personal light frequency.

What if negative patterns, criticisms, thoughts and judgements decrease light.

What if positive thoughts and integrity increases light.

What if life is a continual mirror that reflects back to us what we have created.

What if the different energy vibrations of places and people around us can raise or lower our vibration.

What if true answers can be found in the silence of a quiet mind, walking in nature, serene locations, bathing in water, being still, meditating, sunsets and finding our special heart place.

What if saying the word 'cancel' following a negative thought we had, can rule it out.

What if doing a process of saying 'stop' to a series of thoughts coming into our mind can stop a chattering mind and put the soul back in control.

What if when we see that emotions or thoughts are ruling our life, we realize we need to stop it so we get spirit back in charge.

Twin Flames, Soul Mates And Soul Family

What if a soul splits into two parts of the one soul after leaving source, creating 'Twin Flames'.

What if the two parts of the one soul take different paths of learning. The female half mainly learning through the heart and emotions and the masculine half mainly through analytical logic, creating an entire learning experience for the combined soul. But both also experience incarnations as male and female.

What if Twin Flames incarnate together more frequently in earlier learning incarnations and less often as they progress in evolution to a point where one remains discarnate to assist the energy balancing of the incarnated soul until it graduates from 3D, after which the souls learn together.

What if upon meeting our Twin Flame, we feel a profound connection and unconditional love.

What if unconditional love exists through all eternity between the Twin Flames and is so vast it cannot be defined.

What if when a soul finally graduates from the 3rd dimensional plane, they join with their Twin Flame and both learn together through other dimensions, finally merging as one when universal learning is complete.

What if we each belong to a soul family consisting of many millions of souls.

What if within our soul family, we have a core soul group which includes many soul mates.

What if meeting soul mates from our core soul family can bring feelings of connection, comfort, ease, love, trust or familiarity.

What if we often mistake our soul mates as our Twin Flame because of the amount of love we feel, having forgotten the high level of love that exists between Twin Flames.

What if immense love exists between soul mates to the degree they are willing to play adversarial roles to assist the growth of soul mates.

What if it is possible to briefly meet with our twin flame during this final incarnation if assistance is needed to uncover a deeply embedded situation that no-one else is able to help us with.

What if there are only 12 soul families on Earth.

What if souls and entire soul families are identified by their eternal signature vibration.

Universal Law

What if there are many universal laws that govern the physical universe.

What if it is a violation of the universal law of Non Interference for a more evolved species to alter or assist the evolution of a less evolved species.

What if an exception applies to the universal law of Non Interference if a planet has been invaded by a more evolved species without a broad consent from the species or its universal guardians.

What if the universal law of Non Interference can be put aside if a planet is about to destroy itself or another planet, or is holding up the evolution of a galaxy or section of a galaxy.

What if an addition was added to universal law years ago that prevents nuclear war on Earth, allowed to ensure it did not annihilate itself and cause contaminated debris in space.

What if planets arrange boundary points between them in space to allocate border responsibility.

What if it is a universal violation of the free will of a soul to project healing toward a soul without permission from that soul or its higher self or guardian, or by 100% true knowing it is in divine order to do so and is not an impulse coming from own thoughts, emotions or ego.

What if sending light or healing to someone who has chosen a dark energy path, or does not wish to be healed or where healing is not in divine order for them, is a violation of their free will and can create karma.

What if evolved souls who came to assist Earth to 5D are permitted to use the Universal Right to Decree to speak on behalf of their soul families regarding situations that benefit humanity in divine order.

What if an aware soul who is intuitively guided can use the Universal Right to Decree to request assistance for people and situations, including stating 'where it is in divine order'.

What if a divine decree needs to be stated three times using the exact words (said aloud) without error or having any addition of sound (such as a cough) which keeps it mathematically identical and allows it to placed in the universal records as a decree.

KEY POINTS FROM PREVIOUS CHAPTER

What if it is thought by souls that creates the entire physical universe.

What if our individual thoughts create every interaction, every encounter and every event we experience in all dimensions but the thought is consciously made in higher frequencies.

What if life is a continual mirror that reflects back to us what we have created.

What if always acting in integrity ensures an increase of vibration and lessens the possibility of creating karma.

What if learning on Earth includes realizing that the intentions, thoughts and actions we send out into the world act like a boomerang and are returned as experiences.

What if lessons increase in intensity and frequency until we handle or release what we are being shown.

What if an illness is a sign reflecting a specific underlying thought pattern that needs releasing. See 'You can heal your life' by Louise Hay

What if discernment means having an awareness of the energy of a person, place, object, product, thing, etc. giving us the choice to align with it or not.

What if the reality that receives the most agreement and therefore the most energy, becomes the predominant reality in the life of a soul, nation or planet.

What if detachment, integrity, discipline, responsibility and love are integral to soul advancement.

What if when a soul attains what it needs to learn, it can then stop attracting lessons and starts to attract whatever it prefers.

What if we are in a transitional period where awakened souls move into a void, a period that spans between the soul letting go of the old 3D and moving in vibration to the new 5D frequency, during which period they receive a lot of help from many clear signs showing what they need to handle or release.

I AM

I am the wind and the rain.

I am the sun and all that shines.

I am that which holds the heavens and all that does not shine.

I am the all of all-ness and the no-thing of nothingness.

I am you - the very source of your being.

That which breathes you as you breathe me.

I am that which creates through my breath

and the sounding forth of my words.

I am that which uses care in making myself known to you,

for unto man comes a mighty resistance to claiming me as

I Am That I Am.

For in so doing, one claims the self as I Am That I Am.

I reside in your heart and in your mind.

I reside in the all of you, your fingers and toes, your organs,

your emotions, your thoughts and indeed in your actions.

For good or for naught matters not for I do not judge myself.

I am love, so great and so vast, that I reside

in a state of namelessness and formlessness

for no-thing can I create can contain me, for I Am That I Am.

To limit myself by these very words diminishes my being

by encapsulating my breath,

my words into the world of form.

Each word I speak, in this moment, is creating for I am that

which manifests myself without definition or containment.

As the rock creates a ripple in the pond,

I create ripples with my breath.

Upon each exhale, I send myself forth to materialize

in the world of man through action, through inspiration,

through the very beingness of the hearts of my heart.

If you, who is me, visualize me,

I am not containable in a single form,

or any form for I am un-ending - the alpha and omega.

I have no face or body. I have no religious right or left.

I have no direction.

I possess no correctness

and know not the concept of wrong, of judging,

of being evil or of being good.

If you welcome me into your thinking, feeling, acting body,

you may find that as I am unleashed in the power of one,

who is you, creation is everflowing, unstoppable.

I surround you now in fields and flowers,

stars and comets, rain and thunder.

I surround you now in the suit of skin that cloaks

your bodyworks, your organs and cells and arteries.

I am all that and more.

Yet, often times, you see me not in the workings,

the appearance of all things

for you understand not the mind of God,

which is no mind at all, for I Am Love.

A love so vast it responds immediately to the smallest cry,

the tiniest of whimpers of desire.

If one wishes to experience the thrill of terror,

one will surely find terror on the doorstep.

If one holds the smallest particle of doubt,

doubt will surely appear.

For I hold no limit in my expression.

I Am That I Am.

You have seen me in your lover's eyes

and the tiny fist of a newborn child.

You have seen me in the warships

and in the bloom of a flowering plant.

You have witnessed my phenomenal appearance

with every breath you take,

in the all of which you are surrounded.

You live, move and have your being in me as I, in you.

We are not separate.

I am you.

I am divine perfection.

I am known to you.

I live in you.

I express in you.

I am creator and creation in one.

I am unity.

SOURCE

What if we all are Source/God and are One.

What if Source/God split into billions of parts to experience itself.

What if as Source/God, we are eternal, immortal and infinite.

What if Source and souls are a static state.

What if a soul has no inherent mass or wave length.

What if a soul creates and uses energy, but is not energy.

What if all souls have an inherent ability to perceive and identify energy.

What if every soul is capable of creating anything by knowing it can.

What if Source/God created a physical universe to experience itself.

What if a soul needs to consider itself separate from source/God to be able to experience a universe.

What if a soul never separates from source.

What if every soul has its specific inherent vibration, like its own unique stamp, when it individualises from Source that defines it in the universe.

What if we recognize souls, wherever they appear in the universe, by their own unique vibration.

What if we need to agree to the existence of the physical universe with its component parts of matter, energy, space and time, in order for the universe to exist as a reality for us.

What if the entire universe is an illusion, appearing real only by agreement.

What if when separating from Source, we create the idea we are located so we are able to view and experience the universe.

What if a spiritual being has no actual location and can only consider it is located.

What if there are other universes outside our physical universe.

What if a thought when viewed exactly as created in its own time, place, form and event, duplicates itself and disappears.

What if for a thought or any matter to continue to exist, it has to contain a lie.

What if unwanted situations resolve when viewed in the exact truth of their creation.

What if in order for matter and energy to persist, it cannot be viewed as it is in its moment of creation or it will disappear.

What if energy changes, diminishes, increases and relocates but never vanishes.

What if God/Source is a state of Knowing.

What if when a soul leaves Source, it moves to a state of Not Know to be able to interact and experience the universe.

What if love is an energy vibration adopted by the soul after it leaves Source/God.

What if the light and dark energy existing in duality is created for a soul's experience and growth.

What if learning in 3D and 4D duality could be a game between light and dark.

What if knowing both sides would void the game and prevent the soul obtaining growth from experiences.

What if all spiritual beings are connected through consciousness.

What if humanity has access to a collective field of consciousness.

What if a soul can move freely and instantly anywhere in the universe within its own frequency band.

What if the more evolved the soul, the greater the awareness it has of other realms of existence.

What if souls appear androgynous (no male or female appearance) from the 9th dimension and beyond.

What if we are most comfortable with a specific frequency of light that merges easily with our energy field in that moment.

What if a there is a divine and poetic order of the intertwined relationship of planets, celestial bodies and solar system with vibrational tones creating harmonious and beautiful sounds called the music of the spheres.

What if a cosmic orgasm frequency exists in higher realms.

What if a soul uses mathematics, consciously or unconsciously, to assist life on every level in the physical universe.

What if a soul who chooses to examine the origins of Source/God accidentally erases their agreements to the existence of the physical universe and the universe disappears for them. (See 'If the universe disappears for you.')

What if Source is totally neutral and contains no duality.

What if source by being neutral, with no opposing duality such as love and hate, means love is a creation emanating from thought by Source but is not Source.

What if the entire physical universe is not Source itself, but a thought of creation of matter, energy, space and time that allows experience to be obtained and played out.

THE PHYSICAL UNIVERSE

What if the entire physical universe is composed of matter, energy, space and time.

What if the universe is based in mathematics.

What if every thought, action and energy has a precise mathematical location in the universe.

What if the cycle of the physical universe is create - survive - destroy.

What if the physical universe requires continual motion to persist.

What if the universe keeps expanding in motion by creating more dimensions.

What if there are 12 dimensions and the 13th dimension is nearing completion.

What if many dimensions exist with levels from dense to lighter energy, each level providing a different experience for the growth of the soul.

What if a soul graduates through experiencing levels of each dimension.

What if everything and everyone in the universe is connected.

What if the creation of an effect is the highest purpose of a soul.

What if emotion and thought are stored in subtle energy bodies outside the physical body.

What if the reason for thoughts and emotions is to experience the universe.

What if everything that occurs in the universe is recorded in the etheric realm Akashic Records.

What if every soul's thoughts and actions of each lifetime are recorded in the Akashic Records.

What if there are other universes outside the physical universe that do not contain the same components as the physical universe, e.g. perhaps having only energy.

What if there are several doorways/gateways between the physical universe and entry into the next universe.

What if gateways into the next universe can be located by a soul with sufficient awareness.

What if the universe next to the physical universe operates with a higher form of mathematics.

What if Earth is a planet earning through Limitation.

What if there is life on other planets in the universe, in varying stages of evolution, including the solar system of Earth.

What if multiple timelines exist, each containing different frequencies of reality.

THE CURRENT POSITION OF HUMANITY ON EARTH

What if Earth is in a state of ascension to a higher frequency of light.

What if everything happening on Earth, individually, nationally and globally can be understood when viewed in the context of the Divine Plan goal of the Ascension of Earth.

What if we are creating a bridge of inter-dimensional expansion for humanity, assisting globally to dissolve the old to make way for the new.

What if Earth and humanity are now experiencing in order to reject and release all existing 3D reality.

What if duality and 3D experience is ending on Earth.

What if Earth is shifting in frequency to the band of the 5th dimension.

What if humanity is being offered a choice to move into the divine flow and raise their frequency to 5D.

What if all individuals choosing to either let go of 3D reality and increase their vibration to 5D or continue to experience learning obtained from further incarnations in the 3rd dimension.

What if those choosing to continue with 3D life will do so on another planet beyond this sector of the galaxy because this sector will be in 5D and no longer able to offer 3D experience.

What if everything happening on Earth is an ingenious divine plan to reveal the truth of the existing hidden reality on Earth, allowing the exposure to be experienced by individuals to bring understanding of outcomes when our power is handed to others to make life decisions, and there is little intuition or responsible inspection. The wisdom obtained assists a soul's future path in the universe.

What if Earth's ascension was planned long ago and had pre-arranged agreements due for this exact period, to bring together evolved souls who incarnated as a massive light force, to work in harmony with millions of beings in higher dimensional star systems.

What if all the timelines on Earth have merged into one timeline to allow all reality to be visible. Prior to this people in higher timelines had no awareness of the lower timelines. Ultimately, this unites humanity onto one page of shared reality, to be able to move together.

What if the evolved souls who came to help Earth to 5D processed all the revealed information; analyzing; transmuting the negative energy, emotions and judgements, understanding the higher purpose, accepting the divine outcome and timing of it and passed the result into the human collective for the benefit of all.

What if by collapsing timelines into one reality meant souls who were previously in a higher timeline had a good ability to process newly discovered realities more

What if the existing entire spectrum of reality on Earth is now becoming visible to everyone.

What if the evolution of souls incarnated on Earth now involves the letting go of everything that does not reflect the soul's truth.

What if the processed information that souls pass into the etheric field can lessen the energy of intense negative reactions from humanity, as well as prevent mass negative energy entering Earth's field, should humanity become aware of a world situation that provoked a lot of judgement and negative energy.

What if when a soul rejects a component of society it also lets go of that as a 3D attachment.

What if Earth is releasing the energy of any reality that emits a frequency incompatible with 5D.

What if all areas of society require reviewing by humanity to transmute the dense energy of false data, with law, pharmaceutical, education, big business, TV, media, food industry, social media, governments, internet, religious organizations, Hollywood, music industry, health organizations, charities, orphanages, elections, medical departments, hospitals, governments, goods approval departments, advertising, banking, stock market, shipping, weather, sport and security agencies.

What if covid has helped bring the world together, uniting everyone for the first time in a common situation that affected all regardless of nationality, belief, wealth, culture, gender, religion, status, age, education, profession or social standing.

What if prior to incarnating, souls were aware of the pending covid event and chose their path actions accordingly.

What if covid offered souls a pre-planned departure point to leave the body and enter 5D or enter a new experience on another 3D planet.

What if all 3D patterns ingrained in the human psyche require events to be created that will result in personal experience that encourages reviews and releasing beliefs in order for humanity to transit to a higher frequency.

What if the bulk of food eaten by the majority of humanity is grown or enhanced with artificial chemicals.

What if an upheaval is needed to force a major change in humanity's awareness, fixed beliefs, complacency, addictions, assumptions, habits, patterns and trust in authorities regarding food supplies.

What if we need to release anything we are attached and unwilling to let go of.

What if the bulk of the food industry on Earth uses crops grown with pesticides and will need to be replaced by ethical food production.

What if attachments that need releasing can include habits, ideas, beliefs, patterns, friends, family, routines, music, destinations, identity, TV, teachers, gurus, family, books, goals, places, reading, people, pets, food, social structures, rules and laws, education, gardens, travel, household appliances, emotional reactions, lies, drugs, medicine, complacency, emotions, drama, history, old loves, objects, house, land, colour schemes, furnishings, nationality, religion, ornaments and material things.

For Earth to ascend it has to transmute all dense energy, so humans need to release theirs.

What if ascension means is increasing our light vibration to a point where a higher dimension becomes visible.

What if we ascend when w have gained all learning from 3D and expands consciousness to a level of a higher dimension.

For Earth to ascend it has to transmute all dense energy within its entire field including humans.

What if ascension occurs by increasing our light vibration to a band of light where a higher dimension becomes visible.

What if we ascend when we have gained all possible 3D learning and expanded our consciousness to include a higher dimensional frequency.

What if we are letting go of everything that does not align with our true nature to rise above 3D.

What if we are rising above the limitations of our own reactions, personal ego and the 3D matrix reality of thoughts, beliefs and dense energy.

ADVANCING TO HIGHER DIMENSIONS

What if everything in every area now being revealed on Earth is in divine order to help humanity release 3D reality.

What if a combination of many millions of evolved lightworkers, including the original 144,000 Starseeds, incarnated from different planets and dimensions to assist in raising the frequency on Earth to a 5D level.

What if Earth and humanity are in the process of increasing frequency to a level of the 5th dimension.

What if, with some exceptions, the souls who originally came to help raise Earth's frequency to 5D will return to their dimension, planet or galaxy once their role is complete.

What if many children on Earth are assisting Earth in her ascension to 5D, often by emitting their higher frequency of light and will return home when their work is complete.

What if some children who incarnated to assist the shift to 5D will continue life in 5D.

What if the energy frequency of source is contained in the words starseed, starchild and starchildren, allowing them to tap straight into source during their time on Earth, and this is lost when those words are substituted, e.g. indigo child.

What if higher light frequencies are flooding Earth from higher realms to assist Earth's shift to the 5th dimension.

What if all souls have made, or are making, a choice to move to the higher 5D vibration or continue learning in 3D.

What if depending on a soul's choice to ascend to 5D or not, it can choose to awaken, increase vibration and begin releasing 3D or choose to remain unaware of the planetary changes.

What if without realizing it, souls have begun their personal journey of letting go of Earth's 3D reality.

What if the current upheaval on Earth that is causing shock, trauma, loss, anger, fear, frustration, rejection, aggravation, impatience, pain and suffering, is reality becoming visible to allow it to be rejected, transmuted and released.

What if the extent of shattering humanity's reality on Earth needs to continue in intensity until people see it and choose to let go of 3D.

What if when releasing our agreements and attachments to 3D reality, we start to become our true self as a spiritual being.

What if visualising a gold infinity symbol can seal any energy including disruptive or negative energy emitted from the ground or underground waterways into our home.

What if we have the capability to know the whereabouts and have the codes to unlock stored ancient energy in etheric vaults around the world awaiting this time to be released.

What if this entire sector of the galaxy is entering a 5D frequency.

What if all atomic particles on Earth are quickening in frequency in preparation for Earth's shift to 5D.

What if time is an illusion that exists only in the 3rd and 4th dimensions for soul learning.

What if time appears to be happening because we see a movement of particles.

What if Earth is losing the reality of time because it is shifting to 5D, a frequency band in the present moment and without time.

What if clocks appear the same, but we are losing time and our days seem shorter.

What if we have actually lost 15 hours, 47 minutes and 13 seconds as at 15th March 2024.

What if we need to stop our mind and ego directing life with what we should, need, must and have to do, and instead be intuitive so we are able to function successfully with shorter days.

What if an incarnated soul can adequately sustain the physical body by using a high frequency of light as a food source.

What if we are meant to live on light, it will resonates deeply as necessary for our plan at the right time.

What if each day we are presented with the things in 3D we are still attached to.

What if we need to let go of agreements and attachments to 3D before we can move into a higher frequency of light.

What if fasting can help a soul overcome the need for dense energy food as it transitions to being sustained by a lighter frequency.

What if we are always supported by the universe, whatever path or action we choose.

What if a lightworker is able to request karmic absolution (karma is wiped) which will be granted if in divine order.

What if there is a transitional period happening now where awakened souls are in a major void, which is a period between the soul letting go of the old 3D and before moving into the new 5D frequency, during which they receive a lot of help by being given a surge of many very clear signs showing what they need to handle or release.

What if intuition guides us effortlessly on our path.

What if intuitive guidance will provide the resources, time, money and contacts needed to reach our goals.

What if we prevent intuitive guidance by thinking too much.

What if the energetic vibration of a person, product, thought or location can be beneficial or harmful.

What if we need to be fully awake before we can leave 3D matrix programming.

What if rejecting corruption can clear dense levels of energy from Earth.

What if restricting freedoms in society can help people overcome it and gain mastery.

What if two identical items cannot occupy the same space means that forming a perfect physical or mental duplication in the mind causes a disappearance.

What if the 5th dimension already exists but can only be seen when a soul's own frequency matches that band.

What if it greatly assists a soul to just stop everything and take a moment during the day to become still and align to source.

What if we can greatly expand our awareness by setting aside programmed and adopted beliefs.

What if life is a sequence of synchronistic events to help us attain our goals.

What if observing the synchronicity of events means we are present in the moment in the flow of divine order.

What if a failure to see the synchronicity of events means we are being directed by our thoughts or ego and are missing the moments arranged to assist our life path.

What if ego keeps us in the 3D matrix.

What if judging people creates separation, diminishes light and moves us away from our true self.

What if we continue learning through all dimensions in the universe until we acquire the wisdom that is offered through eternity.

What if most old souls are now permanently ending all 3D incarnations, joining with their Twin Flames and returning home to the higher dimensions (after the end of mission banquet!).

What if all souls have a universal goal to attain unconditional love for all life existing everywhere.

What if personal and collective people power can unite the world and create a new future.

What if a major key for soul growth is to focus on integrity, intuition, love and conscious awareness.

What if unconditional love allows us freedom from 3D.

What if many souls are now spanning between 3D, 4D and 5D, experiencing moments in each dependent on their vibration in the moment.

What if we are experiencing some thoughts that literally vanish in a second, so fast its content can't be retained and it is a sign of the soul in 5D in that moment. Not to be confused with forgetting things 5 minutes later.

What if the light force on Earth has created a blueprint that includes the transmuting of the physical body when the soul ascends to 5D, as opposed to it dying.

What if many light worker souls have been here since Atlantis, actively working, teaching, raising light and setting the scene in preparation for the ascension of Earth and the mass awakening and resumption of power by humanity as Earths frequency is being raised to a 5D level of light.

What if life in the universe is all about Source/God experiencing itself.

What if the third dimension is an illusion, existing only for spiritual experience and growth.

What if the entire universe is an illusion, only existing for spiritual experience and growth.

CHRIST CONSCIOUSNESS

The Christ Consciousness is a level of awareness where you no longer see error in any action that you do or in any other human being but see only the beauty and perfection in all things.

For the Christ Consciousness does not judge, does not criticize, coerce, tempt does not condone, does not react negatively. For the Christ Consciousness is truly only true wisdom, Divine truth, true happiness, unconditional love and total perfection.

You will know when you have reached a level of Consciousness of the Christ when you are in a space where you can smile at every human being that you confront in your life without passing any thought or word of judgment, but look into their eyes, which is truly the mirror of their soul and surpass all outer influences of the human nature to truly see only the beauty that exists in their hearts which is their own Christed Being'.

Crea

THE SOULS JOURNEY FROM SOURCE

The existence of the physical universe is created by Source for the purpose of obtaining experience. Source splits itself into billions of parts and sends out souls with free will and choice to create from thought, manifesting and encountering whatever they choose. The capacity of the soul's imagination is unlimited and unrestricted in what it can create. The entire universe is created from the soul thoughts.

When separating from Source, the soul adopts an apparency of being separate from Source. All souls emerge from Source with equal potential, perception and ability to create. A soul leaving Source needs to consider itself to be 'located' in the physical universe of contains matter, energy, space and time, in order to experience it. So, it adopts a location point to view in the universe it creates.

The soul, being a part of Source, can weaken or strengthen its inherent quantity of source essence by its own thoughts and actions. Thoughts in each moment decide its outcome. If the soul continues to think dense negative thoughts, it weakens the soul and decreases its capacity to function in a strong, independent manner. Those choices keep the soul in fixed patterns of behaviour, making it difficult to see logic or alternate views of events. It results in a weaker soul without the energy or impetus to shift in frequency. A weak soul is likely to remain on the 3D treadmill, unable to escape the false reality around them and so may continue incarnating. That pattern remains until change occurs that propels the soul into awareness. The 'quality' of soul essence always remains.

A soul can be strengthened and raised in vibration by freeing itself of attachments to dense 3D energy realities imbedded in human society, such as negative thoughts, judgements, petty considerations and the endless storylines that revolve around human behaviour and ideas people have of what is 'right' for everyone else. A pure intent and integrity of thought and action merge the soul with higher frequencies and increases its life force quota. The soul also becomes less susceptible to lower frequencies. With increased life force the soul is more powerful; more effective; its capacity and zest for life increases; perception expands; attention shifts from 'self' to the needs of others; capabilities expand; spiritual compassion increases and the soul begins to consciously create life in each moment. The soul becomes aware of a higher picture to all aspects of life and springboards into multi dimensional awareness of higher states of consciousness.

Every individual on Earth is making choices that will lead to the path they experience. Everyone is choosing whether to continue learning in 3D or move to a higher level of experience in 5D. Of course, we don't actually 'move' to 5D, we raise our frequency and 5D becomes visible. There is an incredibly perfect divine plan occurring that encompasses us becoming who we really are and preparing us for transition to 5D. As areas are revealed, realities are exposed that we disagree with. By rejecting that reality we step free of the 3d matrix. Eventually every particle of dense energy that exists in the 3rd dimension will be rejected. Souls work toward a universal goal of unconditional love which incorporates other worlds and life forms in all galaxies.

Dimensions are created to incorporate the soul's ability to create. Nothing is stagnant or motionless in an ever expanding universe. Currently, we have 12 dimensions with a 13th nearing completion. As extensions of Source and in conjunction with Source and with each other, we create the universe ahead of us for our own expansion.

Existence is infinite. You will always exist. You have the same capacity as Source. Source sent you out as part of itself. You are eternal and immortal. Source is unlimited. There are many ideas about who we are and what source is. Maybe it is something we don't know until we are ready to return to source. Senior to everything is free will and choice. Souls are not suddenly swept back into Source or disappear into a mass conscious state. It is a choice made by the soul. You are not needed in that source space for any reason at all, ever. You can continue for multi billions of years (or forever!) having fun, creating amazing new experiences, interacting in wonderful ways with great friends and experience immense levels of love. As a creator you can create whatever you like. You may want to sit in serenity with your twin flame by a beautiful ocean for a hundred years. That would be a nice break after 3D.

You may wonder how a soul can keep expanding and grow wiser and more loving. At this time, humanity is consciously aware of caring for just one body in one location on one planet and even that is not always easy. What if we were aware of all our parallel lives at the same time? So, what is it we can learn in the future in higher dimensions? How about being consciously aware of having 20 bodies, each with different viewpoints, in different lives, on 5 different planets, in various dimensions? How about 1,000 bodies on 50 planets. How about learning to interact with other galaxies, other universes and higher mathematics. How about having a body that is an entire planet (such as Earth/Gaia). Each higher dimension offers different learning for soul growth and the potential for experience is immense.

We need to trust we are not here by accident. Millions of souls came here expressly to enact out this multi dimensional magnificent plan to unravel an entire 3D matrix and help Earth move from dark to light and deception to truth.

The goal of the light force was to assist Earth to ascend, but Earth wants all her life forms to be included in the ascension process. So by association, we are also helping humanity increase its vibration.

Humanity and other evolved animals choose their evolution, but many life forms in nature are linked to the energy field of Earth and so they automatically ascend with the Earth.

People are making choices for their future and need to make them freely and without hindrance or judgement from others. We can enjoy this incredible universal experience from a place of love and detachment, observing the densest energy planet in the universe transmute itself into full light.

The old souls and most other evolved souls who incarnated on Earth to assist her frequency to increase to 5D, will return home to their higher dimension when their individual roles are finished.

We have such an exciting journey ahead for us. The possibilities of wonderful co-creation ahead are endless.

Humanity is letting go of 3D!

IF THE UNIVERSE DISAPPEARS FOR YOU

I am writing this because it happened to me and I could not find any written answers to help. Like all things in the universe, there are no accidents so I was probably not meant to find the answers, perhaps being one of many forging a blueprint for this situation. But that was all some time ago. We are in a new time. We have reached the predestined time for humanity to raise its consciousness to the frequency of the fifth dimension

Although what is described ahead is unlikely to occur as a result of the healing and philosophical practices currently available on Earth, the new focus of people working to raise their consciousness increases chances of new spiritual experiences.

This is not a suggestion to seek this out and is not advised to do so. It is also unlikely to occur, but is being written on the slim chance that if someone was searching deeply into their origins and found their original agreements, then the universe will disappear for them. The soul may also resume their native state at that point. Both require re-entry into the universe.

If this should occur to you, you can re-establish yourself back into the universe by agreeing again that it exists. What you are agreeing to is the existence of matter, energy, space and time. The only way you can re-enter the universe is by agreeing it is real for you. Don't be concerned. The universe is set up to help you.

When you first entered the physical universe, you made agreements to allow you to perceive the universe existed - so you could interact with it. You agreed that matter, energy, space and time existed. You also needed to adopt a point of location so you could view that universe.

When the universe disappears, your viewing point may vanish. It might re-establish itself automatically. If it doesn't, you will need to create a point of location in the universe. You are in creator mode. It is not difficult. Just have the intention to agree it exists and it will happen. It only takes a second. The soul needs to consider it is located. It has nothing to do with the location of your current physical body on Earth. In truth, a spiritual being has no location. It can only consider it is located. The soul never actually separates from source.

Regardless of whether or not anything re-establishes itself automatically, it is useful to understand what just occurred to help you with the changes it produces. If this situation does occur (and you wish to continue with your current life in 3D), you need to understand your vibration increased when you resumed your native state. You are now in creator mode. This may not last for long because you are re-entering 3D. Having your agreements vanish will have thrown you out of a time sequence and into the present moment. Being in the present sort of feels like being in a void. Nothing seems to exist a minute before or a minute after the present moment.

Memories of some things you did in your life without conscious awareness may have disappeared. What do we do that is done without conscious awareness? You may recall times you drove somewhere and arrived at your destination without any idea of how you got there. Those memories will return but may take weeks or months to do so. They reappear as you begin to agree and align again to 3D reality because doing this lowers your vibration. So, a sequence of time and mental image pictures return. You will also be able to create new thoughts without them instantly disappearing. Your spiritual knowing remains intact during this period and this helps carry you through. You may experience unusual things such as not knowing how to drive to a friend's house despite having driven there many times before. You handle this by looking over a map of the route. As you view the streets again, it registers a new creation and you will be able to drive there. You may need to use this re-creating technique for many things.

Upon resumption of your 3D life, you will still be in some level of creator mode. It might take a little while to get back into a more normal mode of life, where thoughts don't disappear as fast as you think them.

There is a reason why thoughts disappear in this situation. You are in the present moment and are being a creator. It is a law of the physical universe that if we think the same exact thought as it was created, it forms a perfect duplication of itself and vanishes. Two identical things cannot occupy the same space. To function successfully in 3D, we need to be able to hold our thoughts. So, to keep a thought in existence, i.e. to have it continue beyond its moment of creation, a lie must be added to it. So, what we do is add a lie to it. We don't do that consciously. It is done on a soul level by assigning 'other authorship' to the thought. In other words, we say it wasn't us who created it. Humans go through life experiencing events in 3D as though they didn't create them. Our house gets robbed but we never realize that in order for that to happen, at some point we have agreed such a thing was possible and so it became part of our reality to experience it. We actually create all of the events in our life. Eventually we reach a stage where 'knowing' replaces thought.

The reason we create something and then forget we created it allows us to grow by overcoming unexpected events that suddenly appear in our life. If we were already aware we had created something, we are unable to learn from it. It is similar to knowing both sides of a game. There is no challenge. No game. For example, let's say that before incarnating you arranged for your husband to leave you without means or money when your children were 2 and 3 years old. Your intention behind this plan was to learn persistence, courage and how to overcome the odds, something you had not succeeding with in previous incarnations. This time you include having small children to help push you to success.

You can imagine what would occur if you knew what was meant to happen. The children would reach the age where you had arranged to be deserted and you'd be saying to your husband, isn't it about time you left? Nothing is going to work when you know what is planned. By the way, the children also agree to be part of this for their own learning. We've heard people wonder why we create difficult situations. It's all about growth.

This information is almost impossible to find written anywhere, so recalling this can save a lot of work if you need to re-establish yourself back in the universe.

OLD AGREEMENTS, VOWS AND DECREES

During the pre-planning of our incarnations we arrange key roles with souls who will share our journey. Even though we often have different purposes and goals, we can arrange events that offer growth to everyone. Most of the agreements we make are standard in most incarnations. They include helping each other enhance different spiritual qualities, address karmic imbalance, assist with areas we have not yet mastered and generally help with increasing growth, wisdom and love. Standard agreement can include helping those who had previously helped us. This is often misunderstood and can seem like one side is doing all the work, when viewed from a 3D perspective.

I heard of one incident that had received a lot of judgement and assumption of extreme laziness of the husband. When I looked at what was occurring, I saw what had prompted this agreement between the two people. In the middle ages a man had contracted leprosy, a serious and often lethal condition. For many long years, his every need was taken care of by a good friend who provided his food, accommodation, water, clothing, bandages, bathed his wounds, applied medicine and gave full time care, all at the expense of the helper's life. In the current life, the person who had leprosy was now a married woman and totally devoted to the needs of her husband, supporting him in every way, including financially. He was the friend who had helped her. She had chosen to repay the great hardship he had suffered by devoting her life to him now. This type of agreement is quite normal. Other family members were ignoring the fact that the wife was quite content and happy to do this, and were very judgemental.

In addition to the standard agreements we make, sometimes we make a different sort of agreement. It is not repaying a favour but a choice to help a particular soul as an act of grace. It is more likely to occur within our core soul group. The agreement can apply to an entire incarnational period, but some contain factors that can alter or end the agreement during the incarnation. An action or a lack of action can change the agreement, or the soul may make a different choice and take a different path.

When we make pre-incarnational agreements, we do so from our higher soul perspective. From that higher view, it is assumed the soul receiving the help will act intuitively, and not make decisions from the mind or ego. This means it is assumed they will be aware and pay attention to signs presented by the universe, will be intuitive, act in their mastery and integrity and continually examine their own actions and reactions to life's situations and handle them when they appear. Problems are not anticipated, expected or foreseen. The agreement is often even seen as a backup plan that may never be needed.

Ahead is an example that shows how a failure to act in the flow can impact someone who made an agreement to help.

A group of souls arrange a forthcoming incarnation. Two souls in the group discuss their important divine roles. One of them expresses the difficulty they have handling pain and feels this could impact severely on their work. The other soul agrees to take on any pain that may arise. It is considered by both parties unlikely the agreement will ever be needed because the soul will act intuitively in the flow.

However, we can now see that once we are incarnated, how easy it is to get caught up in a 3D world and let our thoughts and ego direct many of our decisions. Taking action dictated by thoughts and ego, including blaming others and judging, creates negative energy. So, it becomes increasingly vital to notice signs the universe gives us that reveal any negative energy and karma we have created. Luckily, signs from the universe increase in frequency and intensity until we see it and address our reactions. The final signs from the universe are the toughest. If we understand the usual sequence of signs given that will mean the next stage would be pain in our body. This can lead to death. However, in this case, the soul would not be feeling any pain (because the agreement they made removed it) and by not getting those stronger signs that would push them to look, they can easily assume all their actions are right.

The pain is occurring, it is just not occurring to them. The soul they made the agreement with is feeling it. That soul is now experiencing increasing levels of pain which they believe to be their own. Once incarnated, souls do not recall agreements made. This situation obviously needs to be resolved and the agreement needs to be broken. But how! A great deal of awareness is needed by the soul who agreed to take on the pain. They now need to see the signs the universe will send them to show they made an agreement that now needs to be dissolved. It is not always easy to recognize such signs because the idea we have such an agreement does not easily come to mind. The most practical way we can handle this, is to say a general decree that would cover all such agreements that are not in divine order and no longer serve the soul. There is a suggested decree at the end of this section.

OLD VOWS

Sometimes during an incarnation, we encounter a profound situation so deep or intense it provokes us to make a vow, oath or promise. If unfulfilled, such a vow has the power to remain with us throughout time. Even though we are not consciously aware of a vow we have made, it can definitely affect our life. It can determine whether we take or avoid certain actions, and can distract us away from our real purpose.

However, if we have made a vow that is now causing a problem on our path, the universe will show us signs that it exists, so we can let it go. One such instance occurred to me. Although I am not a Buddhist, for many years I had used a lot of Buddhist colours in my home furnishings, as well as acquiring some sacred Buddhist hangings and peaceful figures of Buddha. I ended up with quite a few. I was aware I had previous lives as a Buddhist and had 'assumed' my love of these items was because I had an affinity with the area. I did not look for any other reason.

Several years ago, I was on a spiritual pilgrimage with a group of lightworkers from around the world who had gathered to do specific spiritual work. I was sitting on a bus next to a girl in our group from the USA. She had some artefacts in a bag she had brought with her, and took out a very old Buddhist necklace. The energy of it hit me. I immediately had a memory of being some sort of leader in a village in Tibet, long ago. A horse rider had entered our village at speed, to warn of a marauding band pillaging and burning down villages, was heading our way. I swiftly called the town people together and instructed them to pack what could be carried easily and to leave quickly. We needed to cross the mountains and leave Tibet. As the villagers gathered their belongings, I walked up on the hill overlooking the village. I was deeply upset and felt we may never return to Tibet. As I watched the people file out of the village with pots and pans clinking on their backs, I made a silent vow. 'I promise I will get you back to your homes.' Although I had made this promise hundreds of years ago that I was still trying to fulfil it. I repeated what I had just seen to the girl who showed me the necklace. From my heart, I said to her 'I need to reach all of these villagers and ask them if they will release me from my vow'. Her reply came as no surprise. She said, 'You can start with me. I was there'. The universe had brought us together so I could become aware of that vow I had carried for so long. In order to reach all the other souls of the village, I used an ability we all have. I used my 'intention' to contact the specific souls on an etheric level. We can create by our intent. I asked all that group of souls, if they would release me from my vow. It was granted by each of them. I felt it. It felt right for me to do it in that way, but there are also other ways to dissolve a vow. We are in a different time frame now on Earth and are able to handle things more quickly.

Another situation I discovered which may seem unreal to many people, but is written for those interested in expanding their thinking to include the source of our spiritual self. As we know, we pre-arrange a discarnate team of guides to assist us in our incarnations. They also help us by focusing our attention to specific areas or dropping in thoughts. So, it can happen that some thoughts we have are not ours. This is OK. Our guides are usually up to date with where we are and know what is needed, so this can be extremely helpful. Especially at times we have a sudden thought when leaving home, to check the cooker is turned off that we have forgotten our phone. Perhaps because I am aware our guides do this, I recognise thoughts that are given to me.

Something had been happening over a period of a couple of months. I had noticed some thoughts coming in were not relevant or helpful. This was clear and unusual and I pay attention. I thought maybe I had inadvertently created a hole in my aura through some negative thinking or action on my part and one or two souls had entered my space through such a hole. However, my handling of that, by strengthening my aura with light, did not stop it. So, I paid particular attention to any signs I was being given. These signs kept drawing me back to the idea of old agreements I had made.

When I search for the reason for something, I try to find the first time it happened. Finding and clearing the first time can erase a whole chain of similar events and all thoughts or emotions connected to it. The first time something occurred is the key. When we first start looking for such things, we usually find more recent things. This is a more comfortable gradient for us, as the first and earlier ones are the toughest. I started by finding more recent ones, but having used this practice for a long time, I can now go straight to the tough stuff. As we know, most things in life with pain, loss or trauma is not easy to confront. None of these things are pleasant to look at. And things in our unconscious awareness were usually buried there by us because they were too uncomfortable to view. Even old forgotten agreements can have some trauma attached. Often trauma was the reason we made the vow in the first place.

I searched and found what I needed to help me handle this. The origin had occurred just after I left Source. For all of us, in order to function and experience in the physical universe, each soul ('apparently' now an individual) has to agree to the existence of a universe. Otherwise it cannot be experienced by that soul. When we first leave source, that agreement is left to the soul to figure out. No help is given. The soul also needs to create the idea of manifesting subtle energy bodies around them so it can experience through these. Subtle bodies include our mental and emotional bodies where we store thoughts and emotions. We can be helped to create this, but it is mostly done on our own. I was having difficulty creating my mental body exactly right. I had managed to create the emotional body OK. Ha, in hindsight, maybe it was not so clever to create the emotional one first, as then I created frustration by my many failed attempts to make a mental body. I hadn't anticipated trouble! I could see other souls around me moving into the physical universe which meant they had successfully created the idea of how to manifest subtle bodies. After trying alone for ages, I finally asked for some help from others, and got it sorted. What did not occur to me at the time, was *to end the agreement with those who helped me*. The result was that agreement still existed now. As we know on Earth at this time, we are all being encouraged to let go of everything that is not in full alignment with the soul. So, these souls I had asked originally to help me were still beholden to our agreement to help me. They had been entering my energy field to show me this so that I would release them from it. Of course, I ended the agreement immediately and expressed my immense heartfelt gratitude. So, that was the reason I had been getting unusual thoughts that didn't feel right. Those lovely souls who had originally helped me were deliberately making things not fit in my world so I would pay attention. Excellent move. We only need to observe and be aware and we can let go of everything.

Another agreement I discovered I had made. Firstly, understand that many lightworkers and all the original Starseeds took on some type of illness or condition as part of their role here. It may have been physical or mental. This was to create a pathway of how to resolve this condition. The path and its resolution would then be added into the Blueprint for Earth's ascension giving people with those conditions a path to follow. I recall many years ago I met five starseeds in one week who had painful knees and were using varying methods to fix it. That gives a choice of many path options in the blueprint. One person is not relied on to create the path, but every person counts. I had taken on and handled several different health conditions in my life. However, there was one area I could not seem to handle, despite trying every avenue conceivable. It had reached critical levels and I decided rather than die, which was imminent, I would take steps to locate and break that particular agreement. That was a big decision and was given a lot of careful thought. We never like to let anyone down and always ponder on the possibility we may be about to find the ultimate handling. There is a protocol to follow to break such an agreement. Become very still and state 3 times 'I align to the highest source of all creation'. Then say clearly and with intent, that you now end that agreement. Be specific with the wording. Name the condition as best you can, perhaps listing the symptoms of it, in case you have been misdiagnosed with a wrong name. Say it several times. This implies you have thought about it and this is what you want. By the way, this is not a casual step we do at the first stage of discomfort. The individual decides what is right, when and if it feels right to opt out.

My stories are to give an idea of how vows may come about and the type of signs we might get to help reveal them. *A decree follows to cover all such vows.*

DECREES

There is a Universal Law called the 'Right to Decree'. This allows Lightworkers to make a request to Divine Consciousness on behalf of their various soul families on Earth. While incarnated on Earth we are able to use this Right being an inhabitant of Earth to ask for God/ Source to act on our behalf to handle a specific situation. It is thought this will generally be used for important matters, such as planetary situations, and not to handle a neighbour's barking dog!

There is a protocol to follow in doing Decrees.

The difference between an affirmation and a decree is that an affirmation is repeating a statement to cause a reprogramming of a belief pattern and a decree is a one off statement or request registered in universal law.

HOW TO DO A DECREE

Before you begin any decree, become still in thought and body and state 3 times 'I align to the highest source of all creation'.

Make sure your feet and hands are not touching (i.e. you are not forming a circle, so then the energy can go out). Providing you are in a clear space when you say a decree, saying it just once (but 3 times through) is sufficient, unlike an affirmation which needs to be said often as we are re-programming our thoughts.

To comply with Universal Law (Holy Trinity - Power of Three) a decree needs to be said aloud 3 times using precisely the same words. It is a mathematical procedure, so if you slip up on any word while saying a decree (or cough or add sounds), it is essential to start again from the beginning of the first run through for it to be effective. It will not work unless done correctly. To avoid making a slip up when saying a decree, read it through once aloud just to make sure you are familiar with the words and their pronunciations.

After the decree has been said 3 times, you complete it by sealing it. You can use the words 'So Be It. So It is. It Is Done'. These sealing words only need to be said once (not 3 times).

A DECREE TO VOID OLD AGREEMENTS AND VOWS THAT NO LONGER SERVE

'By Divine Decree, I Am One with the Source of all Creation, I nullify and void any past vows, agreements, judgements, contracts, oaths or promises I have made, at any time on any level or dimension that are detrimental to my well being and no longer serve me in highest Divine Order, and I hereby notify the I Am Presence of any soul where such an agreement is now void.'

'So Be It. So It Is. It Is Done'. (Say this line ONCE AFTER doing the decree 3 times.)

POSTIVES OF COVID

Kick started a major awakening of humanity

Helped shift people out of stuck patterns and routines

Increased ability to adapt to huge and sudden change

Prepared everyone for bigger changes ahead

Let go of old ideas and adapt to new ways to do things

Helped people realize the treadmill and rat race they were living

United the world for the first time in a common situation affecting all

Allowed time to review our quality of life

Global sense of unity with everyone in the world sharing the same situation

Helped to break down social barriers as all experiencing same circumstances

Opportunity for compassion for others

United the entire world for the first time ever, in a situation affecting all

Dissolved many social barriers between countries

Strengthened many family ties

Realized benefits of working from home

Learning to not judge people

Gave choices to change job or profession

Time for gardening, art, walking, hobbies and other pursuits

Brought up many discussions, viewpoints, ideas and solutions

More free time for family, children, play, trips away and sharing

Gave time to think for ourselves and discover we could

More thought and care given to the elderly, including own parents

Gave time to think about life and direction

People got caravans and motor homes and took the opportunity to travel

Chance to start own business or new career

Opportunity to review control of population

Offered a chance to either auto comply or research

Chance to recognise fears of losing job, friends, family, position and finances

Presented hundreds of thought patterns to be reviewed

Tested self integrity

Chance to release anger, frustration, impatience, despair, annoyance and grief

Opportunity to stand own ground with choices regarding compliance

Created work flexibility and choices for the future to work from home

Home schooling helped parents assess material offered in education curriculum

Showed a new way to educate children in easier, relaxed environment

Showed individuals their levels of blind obedience and compliance with authority

Created fun ways to teach kids at home

Offered opportunity for parents to group hire a teacher for home schooling

Helped many children leave the education system and be home schooled

Learned ingenuity and adaptation to new circumstances

Chance to examine how important to us our job was

Enhanced lives with a new pet for family companionship

Realizing courage to rise above political and physical control

Many in orthodox medicine became natural health practitioners

People tackled and completed DIY projects at home

Time to clean house and repair things

Feeling fulfilled by working as a team against a common challenge

Brought shock, fear, doubt, uncertainty and unpredictability to the surface

New look at house condition and furnishings to replace

Formed new bonds and relationships

Revealed who true friends were

Developed spiritual characteristics

Discovering our rights and learned that rules and mandates are not law

Learned we cannot be forced to self harm by wearing masks

A chance to research Sars2 virus showing 99% recovery and lasting only 2 weeks

Chance to learn about experimental vaccinations and voiding insurance

Noting flu statistics dropped from many thousands to a few hundred during covid

Great chance to acquire knowledge to pass on to others

Cared for quarantined people and helping with shopping

Brought about resolve to stop allowing others to control our life

Let go of need to travel

Gave souls choosing to die a method that would ultimately assist truth to surface

Realized how much we had handed responsibility to others for our life

Realized we cannot be forced to ingest anything harmful

Helped people let go of their fixed 3D positions; changing beliefs, ideas, homes, towns, states, rote patterns, actions, jobs, relationships, family and friends

Discovered that no countries laboratories were able to prove the covid virus existed

Gave us the opportunity to evaluate data and information

Learned we don't need any government or authority qualifications for anything

Let people discover they can be brilliant researchers, analysts, authors, designers, inventors, builders, etc.

Offered a chance for us to trust our awareness over claims by authorities.

A chance to understand the immense value of our innate and intuitive knowledge

Helped us build teams and communities

Exposed government control and false information

Revealed new leaders

Showed the value of growing our own food

Gave an awareness of level of government control

Revealed the misuse of science

Really helped to learn to trust in ourselves and each other.

Taught us the value of working together

Showed us how useful research can be

Taught us to be leaders

Gave us greater understanding of freedom

Impelled us to take action

Showed people the value and love of pets

Better prepared for the future to be more discerning regarding complying with directions that reduce personal freedom.

Realized we don't need to succumb, feel intimidated or fearful when threatened with mandates that have no validity in law.

Increased personal and planetary light as the reactions of dense energy that surfaced could be transmuted gradually into a higher frequency of light all over Earth.

Sandy Stevenson

A PROCLAMATION TO A UNIVERSE OF LIGHT

From a place of stillness -

'I align with the Source of all Creation

and using my Right under Universal Law

I speak on behalf of my human soul family.

I Hereby Proclaim -

The destiny of Earth

is now firmly and irrevocably

placed in the hands of the light force

on all levels and dimensions,

to be held in such a place

until the completion

of the ascension of Earth.

So Be It. It Is Done.'

Sandy Stevenson (Shantarn)

BOOKS WRITTEN BY SANDY STEVENSON

All eBooks are available on all reading platforms in major countries.

Books are written for all those who seek truth. To help make them available to everyone, eBooks are priced around $3.00 US.

ENGLISH

1. The Awakener. Best Seller. Originally in paperback. Now only available as an eBook. Note: 2nd hand copies can be found.

2. All That Is Love (previously a paperback titled 'I Am Here'). Now only available as an eBook. Some paperback books are still available in the UK. Contact email: alisonevegrave@btinternet.com Ph: 01577 830595

3. Q & A - Spirit Way eBook

4. Awakener Articles 1995 - 2021 eBook

5. Ascension Awakening Articles 2022 -2023 eBook

6. Seekers of Higher Truth (this book). eBook and Paperback.

GERMAN

1. Erwachen zum Aufstieg ins Licht (German edition of The Awakener) Paperback

LITHUANIAN

1. Budintojai (Lithuanian edition of All That Is Love) Paperback

LIGHT ASCENSION

Website: https://www.lightascension.com/welcome.html

Email: lightascension5d@gmail.com

GLOSSARY

Aura. A subtle energy protective field around any physical body to reflect the state of the living entity (soul, animal, etc.).

Akashic Records. Contains the entire history of every soul since the dawn of Creation. Records are an encoded vibration in a non-physical 5th dimensional plane.

Angelic Realm. A path of experience available in the physical universe that operates in subtle energy light frequencies. The Angelic Kingdom has the function of administering to the spiritual and emotional needs of both the Human Kingdom and the Elemental Kingdom. The angelic realms include the elemental kingdom of elves, pixies, fairies, giant, dwarfs, goblins, gnomes, brownies, sprites, trolls, imps and leprechauns.

Astral Plane. A lower band of the 4th dimension, similar in appearance to 3D but with slightly lighter energy. Much of this plane contains discarnate beings who cannot or do not wish to incarnate or still believe they are in 3D from a previous incarnation. The plane also contains many negative beings who cause psychic attacks and general mischief and infiltrate souls with weaker auric fields. It is a main source for Ouija boards.

Channelling. The receiving of telepathic thought, energy, emotion, light, healing, concepts or information from a source believed to be outside the person's body or conscious mind. Channelling can occur from a connection to anyone including other 3D incarnated souls, the astral plane and other dimensions. Information received from channelling requires discernment to ascertain truth.

Channel. Can refer to a person with telepathic connections and interaction with non physical beings.

Codes. Mathematical codes are the basis of the physical universe. All souls carry mathematical codes in their energy field. Codes are exchanged with other souls, as well as passed to various locations and sacred sites and into the leyline energy grid of Earth. Souls are not usually aware they carry and exchange codes, with it generally occurring automatically.

Consciousness. Degrees of awareness of self and surroundings. On a spiritual level, it can refer to how deeply you understand yourself, your emotions and the world around you.

Decrees. A Universal Right to Decree used by incarnated lightworkers to act on behalf of their own soul families including requesting assistance from higher realms. A decree needs to be said aloud three times using the same words without error or addition of sound (such as a cough) in order to be mathematically placed in the universal records as a decree. See website articles.

Dimension. A point of perception rather than an actual place to travel to. All dimensions have a bandwidth that ranges from dense to a lighter energy. Souls enter the lower energy band of a dimension and when their consciousness is raised sufficiently they proceed to lighter bands within that dimension. This process continues through the various frequencies of increasingly lighter dimensions. However, dimensions can be entered at any level by a soul whose frequency matches that level.

Third (3D). A physically oriented plane offering experience to an incarnated soul to assist growth by overcoming limitations. In the 3rd dimension, people see themselves as individuals. Rooted in a physical world, people feel it is appropriate to judge others based on the colour of their skin, age, gender, appearance, financial status, etc. The third dimension contains an apparency of daily linear time to assist learning.

Fourth (4D). A dimension where a soul begins to awaken and let go of 3D beliefs. Comparison and judgment still exist but with more 'spiritual' themes. Attention has shifted from pursuits in the material world to gaining knowledge and understanding. 4D contains the apparency of linear time and duality. A soul still uses memory and picture images in order to Know.

Fifth (5D). The first point of Ascension for souls and life forms who are transiting from the 3rd and 4th density. 5D has frequencies ranging from dense to fine, each level offering advancement in consciousness to attain higher levels of ascension. Learning is different than a soul experiences in 3D. 5D involves co-creating new societies and technologies that work with harmony, integrity and a love of all life. It has no duality, time, karma, pain, age, ego, suffering or solid physical body. Beings use light bodies that reflect a unique and identifiable aesthetic appearance that match 5D frequencies.

Sixth (6D). A finer light frequency of conscious awareness where the being has a light body and undertakes further learning in subtle energy frequencies.

Thirteenth (13D) Currently under construction, nearing completion.

Discernment. A gift of spirit perception of energy. An essential requirement to be applied to everything seen or heard in order to establish the energies we wish to align with. See articles on the website.

Ego. The soul personality used to interact with society. Can be a problem if the soul allows it to be dominant in life.

Earth. A planet that has acted as a learning ground for humanity and life, to experience situations through 3rd and 4D density that assist growth, as well as provide an environment for nature's many life forms.

The Elemental Kingdom. Nature spirits that operate in the subtle energy realm of universal creation, responsible for the growth and maintenance of the entire world of nature. Elementals translate thought-forms into physical forms, creating specific forms, whether it is an electron, a biological cell, a flower, tomato, a tree, a valley, a planet or a solar system. Grouped in 4 areas. **Earth**: gnomes, pixies, goblins, brownies, tree people, leprechauns, crystal beings, stone beings, dragons, wood nymphs, sprites and trolls. **Air**: Fairies, elves, sylphs and imps. **Water**: Mermaids and mermen, Undines, water sprites and nymphs; **Fire**: salamanders, Unicorns, dragons. Elementals translate thought-forms into physical forms, creating specific forms, whether it is an electron, a biological cell, a flower, tomato, tree, valley, ocean, planet or a solar system.

Energy field. The etheric field around the soul.

Etheric. A fine spiritual energy in space - the ether - ethereal.

Etheric body. Connects our physical body to higher realms of spiritual existence.

Frequency. A band of energy. Frequency refers to the number of changes, periods or vibrations in a unit of time. The number of cycles that a vibrating object completes in one second is called frequency.

Galactic Federation of Light. A space fleet founded millions of years ago that focuses on the preservation of all life, consisting of 59 fleets of 4,600 ships that assist throughout the galaxy where Earth is located. Some commanders and crew hold parallel lives on Earth at this time.

God Creator Source. Unknown static state.

I Am Presence. A soul's higher individualized presence of God.

Inter-Galactic Federation of Light. An extensive space fleet with huge mother ships the size of a small planet that operates as a complete world providing a full life for its personnel. The fleet is responsible for assisting and protecting all galaxies in the physical universe, including developing new technology and science.

Judgements. Using 3D conditioned belief patterns to define life.

Karma. An energy generated by the intent of mental or physical actions in a current or parallel life (past life) that is not in alignment with the soul, resulting in a need to rebalance energy.

Karmic absolution. Karmic absolution is an act of grace where the soul's karma is balanced without the soul needing to undertake events to balance it. It can be requested at this time by souls who are here to assist Earth's ascension. Absolution is granted if it is in divine order and does not prevent essential learning by the soul. To ask for absolution, be still, align with light and say 'In the name of God, I accept the offer of Karmic Absolution. So be it. It is done.'

Lessons. The physical universe provides many dimensions where a soul is able to create unlimited experiences to assist its growth. A soul chooses what it wishes to gain in an incarnation and plans situations to help gain the qualities it wishes to acquire. Once incarnated the soul forgets what it has planned in order to benefit from overcoming unexpected events that arise. It seeks to recognize where it has difficulty remaining centered and balanced or can be triggered into reactive behaviour.

Leylines. A system of ancient, unseen channels of electromagnetic subtle energy and mathematical codes that form an extensive grid on Earth connecting all vortices. A new expanded leyline system, only 18 inches below the surface, has replaced an older more deeply embedded grid system. Many buildings were knowingly constructed on the leyline system such as ancient megaliths, monuments, sacred sites, churches and other prominent buildings.

Living on light. Refers to the permanent sustaining of a physical body in perfect health by a soul aligned to a high frequency of light (called prana) instead of eating food.

Location. A viewpoint adopted by a soul who has chosen to consider it is located in order to view and interact with the physical universe.

Matrix. Systems and structures in 3D society that keep us bound to traditional ways of living which includes society's norms, cultural expectations, educational institutions and corporate structures.

Overlight. Occasionally an arrangement is made between two souls for a discarnate more evolved soul to merge temporarily to add energy, stamina and expertise to a soul who has an important job in its divine role.

Parallel lives. Refers to all the simultaneous incarnations of a soul, all occurring simultaneously in the present moment. Often called past lives being an easier concept to relate to.

Past lives. Refers to previous incarnations of a soul but in truth all past lives occur simultaneously in the present universal moment.

Physical Universe. A creation of matter, energy, space and time in perfect mathematics for souls to experience growth.

Plane. Another word for dimension.

Reality for individuals. The current beliefs held by an individual.

Reality for humanity. The reality being experienced that currently has the most agreement and therefore the most energy.

Space. A viewpoint of dimension.

Soul. A spiritual being. A static, non-material, no motion spark of source creator. It has no mass or wavelength. It has an ability to postulate anything into existence and create whatever it chooses. It has the ability to perceive energy. It has free will to choose any path to gain experience.

Soul family. There are 12 soul families. A soul family consists of multi millions of spiritual beings. A soul feels most comfortable with its own family, although they may have roles as friends or adversaries. We can interact with souls outside our soul family, but are not usually comfortable with the different energy vibration. We plan the roles to be taken during an incarnation within our soul family. Healing circles work better if all are from the same soul family.

Soul family core group. Within our soul family there is a core group, which includes many soul mates. Major roles in a lifetime are usually made with our core group.

Soul mate. Souls have many soul mates who often share a life by taking roles of either gender, such as parents, partners, friends, children, etc.

Soul fragment. An incarnated soul is able to leave a fragment of itself in a location where it wishes to know the outcome of a situation. Sometimes this occurs following death or when a soul is leaving an area and wants to monitor the situation.

Spiritual abilities attained in 3D. Some abilities one can gain from 3D experience is love, joy, compassion, deep emotional feelings, magical moments, friendship, loyalty, trust, humility, motivation, determination, enthusiasm, helping, integrity, truth, heroism, companionship, courage, social interaction and dependence, decisions, non attachment, courtesy, humour, faith, sensitivity, relationships, inspiring others, discipline, kindness, practicality, accountability, change, understanding, silence, goodwill, generosity, awareness, acceptance, tolerance, innocence, flexibility, forgiveness, happiness, wisdom, modesty, respect, positivity, selflessness, right action, maturity, co-operation, devotion, determination, perseverance, power, creativity, affection, aspiration, care, thoughtfulness, freedom and non judgement.

Subtle energy. Subtle energy operates on the principle of resonance. Through resonance, subtle energy can be positively or negatively influenced, affecting our overall well-being.

Time. An illusion that space, particles and motion are real. Time allows a soul to postulate a creation and then forget they did. That illusion is assisted by the apparent passing of time between the moment of the thought and it manifesting, which allows the soul to learn from unexpected events.

Twin Flame. Our eternal other half. As a male and female energy they enter the universe to gain experience. One learns mainly through the logical analytical side and the other through the heart and love. The end result is a perfect balance of heart and logic before joining as one. Unconditional Love exists between the twins. Each half also has incarnations on the opposite path to learn to integrate male and female energy within itself.

Universal Law. The many laws in the universe that govern spiritual conduct in the physical universe. Examples are the Law of Cause and Effect, the Law of Non Interference, The Law of Resistance, The Law of Attraction.

Vibrational essences. Specialized forms of subtle energy frequencies that are placed into liquid, using combinations of mathematics, colour and sound that can positively affect, nurture, feed, repair, sooth, guard, protect, soften and facilitate the expansion of energetic systems that may be out of balance.

Vibration. Refers to the oscillations of the motion of particles. An increase of empathy, love, feeling positive, joy and gratitude can increase personal vibration.

Viewpoint. A soul adopts a point or location so it has a perspective to view the physical universe so it can experience it.

Vortex. A swirling energy point located at key positions in the leyline grid system that runs inside the earth, vital for the functioning of Earth. There are hundreds of thousands of small vortexes (vortices) all over the world and a number of major multi-dimensional vortexes that cover all continents that allow for inter-dimensional travel for all realms of existence including spiritual beings and space craft.

Vortices. Plural of vortex.

BIOGRAPHY

Born in Australia, I spent many years in the UK, travelling extensively around the world, experiencing amazing adventures, places and people. Many special moments include crossing the Sahara and Africa, travelling across the USA in a motor home, winter travel through Europe, camel riding in Egypt, the midnight sun in the icebergs in Greenland, Zimbabwe Falls, northern lights in Alaska and surviving a hurricane in the North Atlantic as ship crew. In 2004, I left my UK Victorian countryside home to live by the ocean in Queensland, Australia. I feel so blessed for my life, for my beautiful daughter and brother and the incredible friends who have shared my journey.

I spent many years devoted to study of the human spirit. My spiritual journey has offered many challenges but I have always searched for the positives and used these as learning opportunities to help me with more understanding of a higher overall picture. I help wherever it feels right and believe that is the reason we came here.

My bestseller 'The Awakener' was a handbook for all who came to help Earth with her transition to a higher frequency of light. It has also been translated into German and Lithuanian.

The second book, 'All that is love' was written as a story and intended to provide a book to assist lightworkers with acceptable, easy to read information to help their friends and family discover their spiritual path. It is a magical, life-changing story about a special group of nine travellers who set out to create a better world by offering a different and exciting way to look at life.

Two further books cover all the articles I have written since publishing 'The Awakener' in 1997. Their titles are 'The Awakener Articles 1995-2021' and 'Ascension Awakening Articles 2022-2023'.

Another book called 'Q and A - Spirit Way' is a compilation of many of the questions I have been asked over 40 years.

Another book is pending in 2025 that may contain a hundred or so images with spiritual messages I have created over many years.

The new book 'Seekers of Higher Truth' is to help give a better understanding of our journey from the point we came from Source and our goals in the universe. It is available as an eBook and paperback.

What an amazing and unique journey we all share.

Many on Earth are coming to the end of a 3D world

where they experienced growth in wisdom and understanding

and are now at the beginning of a new realm of existence

in the higher frequencies of light

that offers growth through beauty, harmony,

peaceful co-existence and serenity.

A world of joy and love awaits.